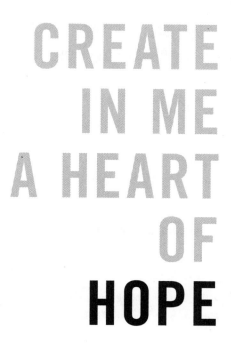

CREATE
IN ME
A HEART
OF
HOPE

Other Books from the (in)courage Community

DEVOTIONALS

Take Heart: 100 Devotions to Seeing God When Life's Not Okay

Empowered: More of Him for All of You

TRADE BOOKS

The Simple Difference by Becky Keife

BIBLE STUDIES

Courageous Simplicity: Living in the Simple Abundance of Jesus

Courageous Joy: Delight in God through Every Season

Courageous Influence: Embrace the Way God Made You for Impact

Courageous Kindness: Live the Simple Difference Right Where You Are

Create in Me a Heart of Hope

Create in Me a Heart of Peace (available August 2022)

Create in Me a Heart of Wisdom (available January 2023)

Create in Me a Heart of Mercy (available May 2023)

For more resources, visit incourage.me

AN
(in)courage
BIBLE STUDY

CREATE IN ME A HEART OF HOPE

Mary Carver and the
(in)courage Community

Revell
a division of Baker Publishing Group
Grand Rapids, Michigan

© 2022 by Dayspring Cards, Inc.

Published by Revell
a division of Baker Publishing Group
PO Box 6287, Grand Rapids, MI 49516-6287
www.revellbooks.com

Printed in the United States of America

Library of Congress Cataloging-in-Publication Data
Title: Create in me a heart of hope.
Description: Grand Rapids, MI : Revell, a division of Baker Publishing Group, [2022]
Identifiers: LCCN 2021020303 | ISBN 9780800738112 | ISBN 9781493434299 (ebook)
Subjects: LCSH: Hope—Religious aspects—Christianity—Miscellanea. | Hope—Biblical teaching.
Classification: LCC BV4638 .C74 2022 | DDC 248.4—dc23
LC record available at https://lccn.loc.gov/2021020303

22 23 24 25 26 27 28   7 6 5 4 3 2 1

CONTENTS

Introduction   7

WEEK 1
What Is Hope?   11

WEEK 2
Hope When You're Waiting   43

WEEK 3
Hope When You're Hurt   75

WEEK 4
Hope When You're Overwhelmed   107

WEEK 5
Hope When You Feel Trapped   139

WEEK 6
The Difference Hope Makes   169

Notes   *199*
About the Authors   *201*

INTRODUCTION

Have you ever felt hopeless?

Perhaps you've found yourself facing circumstances you never prepared for or even imagined, and while you're desperately longing for some help or encouragement, you're beginning to wonder if that will ever happen. Perhaps you've gone through something painful, and now, on the other side, you fear that experience has redefined you or redrawn your perspective in a way that has destroyed your belief in a greater good. Maybe you're looking for any sign of hope, any hint of encouragement, any inkling that this—whatever your *this* might be— won't last forever and won't get the best of you. Maybe you're afraid to hope, or perhaps you're not even sure what hope is.

God's Word and this Bible study are here to meet you in that very place.

For the next six weeks, we're going to dive deep into Scripture to examine what we believe about hope. We'll look at how God offers us hope—real, certain, unshakable hope—when we're waiting and when we're overwhelmed, when we've been hurt and when we feel trapped. Looking at where that hope comes from and what it looks like in our lives will help us understand what hope is and what difference it makes. It will allow God to create in us a heart of hope.

Welcome to *Create in Me a Heart of Hope*. Our prayer is that this study will encourage you to seek the Lord and the hope He offers each one of us—hope in the One who created the universe, including you, and who promises to never leave you and to someday make all things right again.

How to Use This Study

Create in Me a Heart of Hope is designed to be used by individuals or small groups. For groups doing this study, we recommend allowing at least forty-five minutes for discussion (or more for larger groups). Enhance your community study experience with our *Create in Me a Heart of Hope Leader Guide*. Go to www.incourage.me/leaderguides to download your free small group resources.

As you're working through this study, we encourage you to take your time. We believe God has an incredible message for each one of us in His Word, and we will find it when we seek to learn more and go deeper into Scripture. Our prayer is that, instead of being one more thing on your to-do list, this study can be an encouraging, life-giving experience that brings you closer to God and leaves you feeling more peace, stronger faith, and of course, hope.

So work through this study at your own pace. Ask God to reveal His insight and truth to you. Then listen as He speaks to you through His Word.

Each week of this study will begin with a personal story from an (in)courage contributor, following our habit of "going first" with our hard, messy, real stories. Many of those stories begin in deep heartache but inevitably find their way back to God and the great gift of hope He's given us. Each week will also provide a memory verse to work on throughout the study, to empower you with the tools that will keep you grounded in hope long after you close this book. As you go through this study, you will find it helpful to have a Bible and/or a Bible app for reading Scripture, as well as a journal for writing each week's memory verses. (That journal doesn't have to be anything fancy, though. A simple notebook will work just fine!)

The first day of each week will focus on one personal story and introduce that week's memory verse. The following four days will dive deep into God's Word, illustrating the different reasons we need hope, where we can find it, and the difference it will make in our lives.

Are you ready? We at (in)courage are so excited to go on this journey with you! Join us as we examine what God has to teach us about hope and the way He's providing everything we need to face anything this world gives us with peace, confidence, and strength. Join us as we ask God to create in us a heart of hope.

WHAT IS HOPE?

DAY 1

What *is* hope?

Is it merely wishing for something good to happen? Or crossing our fingers and doing our best to will into existence the outcome we desire? Is hope holding our breath while we wait for an answer, saying what we want as an attempt to force that thing to become reality, or refusing to speak our deepest desires out loud in case that prevents them from happening? Or is it the security we feel when our bank account reaches a certain number, our children get into a certain school, or we finally get that promotion at work?

Those are certainly some of the many places the world finds what it calls hope. But not one of them is lasting; not one of them will change your heart and your life, even if your most difficult circumstances stay the same. On the other hand, biblical hope is faithful, indestructible, life-changing, and a gift from a loving, powerful God. As we begin this study about hope, we're going to first take a look at how the Bible defines it. Let's get started!

A Story of Hope

Nobody calls with good news in the middle of the night. My normally innocent ringtone turned ominous the moment it broke the silence and woke me from a sound sleep. After being startled awake in that manner, I wasn't even surprised to hear sobbing when I finally answered the call.

My friend apologized—for calling in the middle of the night and for crying so hard her words were incoherent at first. I assured her that it was okay, that I was there for her. I told her she wasn't alone, and I told her to breathe. Gently, I asked her what was wrong.

Eventually she was able to speak, and in between sobs she told me what had happened. She was shocked and disoriented; she felt betrayed and scared. After a long pause, she finally asked me, "What do I do now? How will I sleep tonight? How can I wake up tomorrow?"

Bleary-eyed and heartbroken, I wasn't sure what to tell my dear friend. I didn't know how to help in that moment. Solidarity and encouraging words only go so far, especially in the immediate aftermath of trauma. And while I could identify with parts of her story, I'd never walked in her exact shoes. Holding my phone with one hand and my head with the other, I silently asked the One who has the answers.

"What does she do now, God? What do *I* do? How can I help her? What do I say? What will even help her right now?"

That was when my friend asked me a different question. She asked me if it would all work out. She asked me to tell her that it would be okay. And finally I had something I could hold on to and then offer back to her. *Yes!* I told her. Eventually, I promised, everything would work out. Someday, I assured her, she would realize that she had healed, grown, moved on enough to feel okay again. I made sure to emphasize *eventually* and *someday*, knowing that my friend would feel the sting of this situation for quite a while. But in that moment, we both felt a glimmer of hope, and it was enough.

She felt a glimmer of hope that, while she was blinded with pain in this moment, it would not last forever. I felt hope that I would not fail my friend in her time of grief, that I could be an encouragement to her.

As my friend continued to cry and process her pain, I thought back to the last time my own world crashed down around me. I could see myself in that moment, falling to my knees on my bedroom floor. Doubled over with sobs I could not control, I felt completely unmoored. Both my emotions and my body felt like they were caught in a storm, whipping from one place or thought to another. Eyes wild and so full of tears I couldn't see, I wrapped my arms around my midsection, wishing desperately someone else could give me a hug, could sit with me, could give me any comfort at all.

When I had felt as devastated and desperate as my friend who called that night, I wanted so badly to know that I wasn't alone. I wasn't naïve; I knew what had happened would have significant, long-lasting consequences. I felt certain I'd be recovering for quite a long time and that recovery would require hard work, strength, courage, and patience I wasn't sure I possessed. But still, I wanted someone to tell me that someday things would be okay again.

As I mentally clawed for any promise or reassurance to wrap my heart around, I felt that same glimmer of hope. Though it didn't occur to me to call a friend to help me in that moment, God got through to me anyway. He reminded me that I wasn't alone and that it would be okay. He pulled His promises from the recesses of my brain to the forefront of my mind, and finally my tears began to subside and my heartbeat began to slow. I remembered . . .

> God is with the brokenhearted.
> He will never leave us. Never.
> He will fight for me. He will win.
> God will work everything out for good.
> He will redeem it all.

During my bedroom floor breakdown and in my friend's moment of crisis, it was hope that saved us. It was hope that helped us make it through the next minute, the next day, our entire lives after heartbreak. Hope is what kept both of us from being completely submerged in despair, from giving up entirely. It's what helped us eventually stand up—even while we still cried, even while we still hurt—and face whatever would come next. Knowing that we were not alone and that God would help us made all the difference.

Without hope, the pain of this world can easily overwhelm us. Whether our strength is sapped by one sweeping blow or it is slowly bled by a thousand seemingly small cuts, we are done for if we aren't wrapped in the hope of God's presence. We must anchor ourselves to His promises to never leave us, to go before us in battle, to love us no matter what, to wipe away our every tear. Without that hope, we are lost.

But with it? With hope in the Lord and His love and power and mercy? Then I know we can make it. With hope, we can withstand the storm and keep pressing forward. We can face every middle-of-the-night phone call and every circumstance that knocks the wind right out of us. With hope, we know *someday* is coming.

—MARY CARVER

Have you ever received a call from a friend in crisis? How did you help them?

_____

_____

_____

_____

Think back to the last time you felt deep heartbreak or pain. In hindsight, what did you need most in that moment? Did you receive it?

_____

_____

_____

_____

In Psalm 62, the author, David, reminds himself that his hope comes only from the Lord. Read the psalm. Why is David so confident of his hope in God?

As we begin this study, take some time to reflect on where you find your security and hope for the future. Write your thoughts here.

SCRIPTURE MEMORY MOMENT

This week's memory verses are Psalm 62:5–6. Write out the verses in your journal (from the CSB as printed here or from your favorite translation). Throughout the week, commit these words to memory as you ask God to create in you a heart of hope.

Rest in God alone, my soul,
for my hope comes from him.
He alone is my rock and my salvation,
my stronghold; I will not be shaken.

A PRAYER FOR TODAY

DEAR GOD, *I need hope. I need a secure foundation to build my faith and my life on. I need something to hold on to when the storms of this life threaten to knock me down. Thank You for promising to be my hope. I ask You to work in me as I go through this study. Show me the truth of Your promises. Create in me a heart of hope that clings to You in all seasons, relies on You and You only, and points others back to You when they face their own challenges. Amen.*

Therefore we do not give up. Even though our outer person is being destroyed, our inner person is being renewed day by day. For our momentary light affliction is producing for us an absolutely incomparable eternal weight of glory. So we do not focus on what is seen, but on what is unseen. For what is seen is temporary, but what is unseen is eternal.

2 Corinthians 4:16–18

What does *hope* mean to you?

We use the word *hope* a lot, don't we?

"I hope you get the job!"

"Hopefully you'll feel better tomorrow!"

"I hope the music is good at church today."

But when it comes to biblical hope, the kind God offers us and creates in our hearts, the definition isn't quite the same as the wishful thinking we express so frequently. In fact, rather than communicating a desire for a specific outcome without any guarantee it will happen, biblical hope is about rock-solid belief in something that simply hasn't happened yet or that cannot be seen by our human eyes.

The original Hebrew word for hope that's used most frequently in the Old Testament is *qavah*, and it can mean "to trust," "to wait," or "to endure."[1] For example, when the prophet Jeremiah cries out to God, asking Him to help the nation of Israel during a devastating drought, he ends his prayer by proclaiming his trust in God and his determination to wait for God's provision:

> For your name's sake, don't despise us.
> Don't disdain your glorious throne.
> Remember your covenant with us;
> do not break it.
> Can any of the worthless idols of the nations bring rain?
> Or can the skies alone give showers?
> Are you not the Lord our God?
> We therefore put our *hope* in you,
> for you have done all these things. (Jer. 14:21–22)

Jeremiah trusts in God's love for His people ("remember your covenant with us") and in God's power ("you have done all these things"), and that allows him to also place his hope in God for help. Throughout the Bible we are urged to hope *in* and to hope *for*. Hoping in something or someone indicates where we put our trust or where we find our security, and we see this all over the Old Testament as God's people cry out for rescue and relief.

Read Psalms 42:11; 119:114; 146:5; and 147:11. Where did the psalmists place their hope? Describe the difference that hope made in their lives. (Read the rest of Psalms 42 and 146 for context around these descriptions of hope.)

In what do you put your hope (or trust) when you are struggling or in pain? If you put your hope in God, what difference has that made for you?

When we turn to the New Testament, we see a slightly different perspective on hope. Jesus changes everything, giving believers a fuller understanding of the eternal hope God offers through salvation. And again, we're not using the word *hope* like the world does, as something we want but don't know if we'll get. Rather, biblical hope for salvation means we have firm confidence in and look forward to the eternal life God has promised through Jesus, regardless of our current circumstances.

Today's key Scripture comes from the book of 2 Corinthians, a letter the apostle Paul wrote to the church in Corinth. Writing from a place of far more suffering and struggle than security and success, Paul

Biblical hope for salvation means we have firm confidence in and look forward to the eternal life God has promised through Jesus, regardless of our current circumstances.

explains in 2:16–18 how he made it through his most difficult days: he placed his hope in the "absolutely incomparable eternal weight of glory" of redemption and eternal salvation in Christ. Though Paul's hope was in something he could not physically see, it more than made up for the great pain he endured on earth.

While that's helpful, it can be easy for us to talk back to Paul and assume he couldn't possibly have understood the troubles we're facing today. After all, what did Paul know of cancer? Or divorce? Or unemployment? Or bullying or comparison or emptiness or overwhelm? What did he know of PTA meetings and soccer games and aging parents and deadlines and workplace harassment and the fear and anger that at times consume our communities?

Perhaps Paul didn't know about the specific things that plague us today—the ones that leave us feeling breathless and beaten down, the ones that steal our joy and leave us pessimistic and, yes, hopeless. But that doesn't mean Paul didn't understand the universal experience of breathtaking disappointment and crushing discouragement. In fact, in the opening paragraphs of 2 Corinthians, Paul writes about how God comforts us in our afflictions, enabling us to then comfort others—and he makes it clear how deeply he understands that on a personal level.

> **Read 2 Corinthians 1:3–11. Pay attention to verses 8–9, where Paul describes just how afflicted and overwhelmed he had been. How did Paul respond to his troubles? How did that affect his trust and hope in God?**

Paul models for us how to live through excruciating circumstances while still maintaining our hope in God's provision for today and our hope for eternity with Him in the future. He acknowledges how hard this life can be: "We don't want you to be unaware, brothers and sisters, of our affliction that took place in Asia. We were completely overwhelmed—beyond our strength—so that we even despaired of life itself" (2 Cor. 1:8). But then he points us to hope as the solution for enduring and moving forward: "He has delivered us from such a terrible death, and he will deliver us. We have put our hope in him that he will deliver us again" (1:10).

Theologian John Piper says, "Hope is faith in future tense."[2] What are you hoping for in the future?

How does defining hope change your perspective on what's currently happening in your life and in the world?

During these next six weeks, we'll discover that hope is not a single-faceted issue that can be simply defined or thoroughly understood in one sitting. But we'll also discover that hope is vital to our faith journey. It's one of God's greatest gifts to our hearts! So get ready to study

God's Word and reflect on all the layers and angles of hope—what it is, where it comes from, how it applies to our lives in various seasons, and what difference it makes.

As you work through this study and allow God to work in your heart, my prayer for you is that you would allow God to surround you with His love and assure you of His promises so you can rest in the knowledge that He is with you and He is preparing a future for you. My prayer is that your hope in the Lord and for eternity with Him will grow immeasurably deeper and stronger over the next six weeks and beyond.

SCRIPTURE MEMORY MOMENT

Read Psalm 62:5–6 and write it three times in your journal. How does understanding more about hope change the meaning of this passage for you?

A PRAYER FOR TODAY

GOD, *thank You for being my hope and for giving me hope. Please be with me as I go through this study. Open my eyes and my heart to better understand the hope You offer, and create in me a heart full of that hope. In Jesus's name, amen.*

Blessed be the LORD,
for he has wondrously shown his faithful love to me
in a city under siege.
In my alarm I said,
"I am cut off from your sight."
But you heard the sound of my pleading
when I cried to you for help.
Love the LORD, all his faithful ones.
The LORD protects the loyal,
but fully repays the arrogant.
Be strong, and let your heart be courageous,
all you who put your hope in the LORD.

Psalm 31:21-24

When you find yourself in the midst of crisis, what is your first response? Do you immediately feel confident of God's help, or do you panic first, like the psalmist in the passage above?

_____

_____

_____

_____

David is the author of Psalm 31 (and many others), but it's unclear at what point during his life he penned these words. What we know of David's life, though, is that it was a roller coaster of triumphs and tragedies. Despite his incredible ascent from shepherd to king of Israel,

David frequently fell victim to the pride and sin of his enemies, his family, and himself. As a result, David was persecuted and betrayed by not only foreign kingdoms but also by his father-in-law and mentor and even by his own son.

It's no surprise, then, that the book of Psalms is full of prayers, laments, and cries for deliverance (along with praise, thanksgiving, and prophecy). And weaving its way through Psalms like a golden thread is the theme of hope. In good times and bad, in seasons of darkness and of plenty, the psalmists consistently come back to the comfort and security they find by placing their hope in the Lord. Hope is what anchors us through the ups and downs of our lives—even when those peaks and valleys are as dramatic as David's.

Regardless of when David wrote Psalm 31, it resonates with anyone who needs protection—either from a situation or from oneself or both. In fact, this psalm is so relatable that portions of it are quoted or alluded to many times throughout the remainder of Scripture. Jonah, Jeremiah, Paul, and even Jesus Himself refer back to these poignant words of David. Needing hope when facing formidable foes is a universal feeling.

While I suspect you haven't found yourself literally swallowed by a whale, hunted by a jealous king, or crucified on a cross, odds are good that you have felt overwhelmed, scared, or unfairly accused. And when your trial or adversary feels as big and formidable as a whale or the ruler of a powerful nation, those situations can make a person lose hope. But David's words in this psalm remind us that even when we falter, even when we panic and lose our footing for a bit, God remains faithful and will secure our hearts and minds in hope whenever we turn to Him.

Read Psalm 31. In verses 21–22, what does David admit he said and believed when he was first attacked? How did God respond when David then turned to Him for help?

Many of us don't immediately turn to God when disaster strikes. But when we do, He's always there. When you've turned to God for help, whether it was right away or eventually, how did that affect your sense of security or strength in that situation?

When life throws us for a loop and we feel like we're flapping about in the wind, often our initial response is to grab anything that seems solid and that we can get our hands on. Like David, we sometimes assume that God has abandoned us and it's therefore up to us to anchor our soul. We give in to the impulse to find something, *anything* stronger than the storm. We look frantically for the thing that will reassure us that everything is going to be okay.

Have you ever panicked and put your hope in something other than God? It feels harsh when David refers to "worthless idols" in verse 6, but that's exactly where we put our hope at times, isn't it? We don't see God at work or feel His presence when life gets hard, so we stop building on the foundation of hope He's offered us and instead place our hope in our savings accounts, in promises from people, in our own determination, in our doctors or pastors, or in abstract ideas like luck or karma.

But hoping in anything other than God will always disappoint us. Hebrews 13:8 tells us, "Jesus Christ is the same yesterday, today, and forever." Only the Lord—never changing, always faithful—is a strong enough foundation to withstand any storm, and our hope in Him is the only hope that lasts. As Charles Spurgeon said in a sermon on Psalm 31, "We are men of great expectations; but our expectations are not in men that die, or men that live, our expectations are in him who never dies, and never fails, and never disappoints those who put their trust in him."[3]

Read Matthew 7:24–27. What happened to the house built on flimsy, fleeting foundations? What "sand" have you been building your foundation on? In what have you placed your hope or expectations? (For example, are you building your foundation on or placing your hope in your retirement savings? Your ability to work hard? Your reputation, your children's accomplishments, or your belief that good things come to those who wait?)

As David brings Psalm 31 to a close, he finds such comfort and relief in God's provision and protection that he urges others to do what he's learned to do: love God, be strong, be courageous. But he acknowledges that this is only possible for those who "hope in the LORD" (v. 24).

It's evident to David, as it will become to us as we study God's Word, that having hope in the Lord is what allows us to be strong and courageous. Hope in the Lord reminds us that we're not alone—so we can be strong even when we face immense challenges. And God-given hope assures us that God will be with us—so we can bravely move forward, even in uncertain situations.

God-given hope assures us that God will be with us—so we can bravely move forward, even in uncertain situations.

May God create in us a heart of hope that consistently turns to Him during times of trouble. May He create in us a heart that leans on and builds upon the solid Rock of Christ Jesus.

What situation are you facing today that requires hope? How would placing your hope in God and only God change your perspective?

_____

_____

_____

_____

_____

_____

SCRIPTURE MEMORY MOMENT

Read Psalm 62:5–6 and write the verses in your journal. Consider how this passage fits with today's psalm.

A PRAYER FOR TODAY

DEAR GOD, *forgive me. I have placed my hope in so many people and things, desperate for something to hold on to, somewhere to find comfort and assurance. But I remember now that You are the only One who can offer me true hope. You are the only One who never ends and never stops loving me. Help me rebuild my faith on the foundation of You and You alone, Lord. Amen.*

Now may the God of hope fill you with all joy and peace as
you believe so that you may overflow with hope by the power
of the Holy Spirit.

Romans 15:13

**Think of a time when you felt overwhelmed or frustrated to the point of
hopelessness. What was it that helped you climb out of that dark place?
Where did you turn to for hope?**

This week's memory verses from Psalm 62:5–6 claim that our hope is
found in God and God alone. And on this side of the resurrection of
Jesus, we now understand that God is a triune God—Father, Son, and
Holy Spirit.

Out of His love and generosity, God the Father offers us hope through
His living Word and His faithfulness in our lives. But He doesn't stop
there. God also gives us hope through the saving power of Jesus and
the comfort and peace of the Holy Spirit. In today's study we'll examine

what the Bible says about how each person of the Trinity fills us with hope.

Let's first look at the hope we receive from God the Father.

In Psalm 62, David says,

> Rest in God alone, my soul,
> for my hope comes from him.
> He alone is my rock and my salvation,
> my stronghold; I will not be shaken.
> My salvation and glory depend on God, my strong rock.
> My refuge is in God.
> Trust in him at all times, you people;
> pour out your hearts before him.
> God is our refuge. (vv. 5–8)

As we discussed yesterday, God is our foundation, and because He will not be shaken, neither will we when we hope in Him. This isn't the only psalm that tells the story of believers finding their hope in God, however. In Psalm 33, the author praises God, recounts His creation of the entire world, and gives Him honor for His unchanging plans and unfailing love. In verse 4 he writes, "For the word of the LORD holds true, and we can trust everything he does" (NLT), reminding us that we can find our hope in God's Word because it is never-changing, accurate, and trustworthy. The psalm then ends with these words:

> We put our hope in the LORD.
>   He is our help and our shield.
> In him our hearts rejoice,
>   for we trust in his holy name.
> Let your unfailing love surround us, LORD,
>   for our hope is in you alone. (vv. 20–22 NLT)

Read Psalm 130. What characteristics or actions of God give this psalmist hope? How is this similar to or different from what we read in Psalm 33?

What does it mean for you to look for hope in God's name or in His Word? Describe the steps you have taken or could take to find your hope in those places. (If you're not sure, know that you've already started by committing God's Word to memory!)

The authors of the Old Testament expressed great hope in the Lord, pointing to His holy name, His Word, and His long history of creation and protection as their reasons for hope in Him. But because they did not know Jesus and had not received the Holy Spirit, they had a limited understanding of who God is. God's people in the Old Testament were required to adhere to the Law of Moses and to make sacrifices on their own behalf to stay in right relationship with God. Not so for us!

Like the classic hymn says, our "hope is built on nothing less than Jesus' blood and righteousness."[4] As Christians, our hope is in salvation through Jesus Christ, the Son of God. Because Jesus died for our sins, our debt is paid and we get to spend eternity with God. No matter how hard our current situation might be, our hope comes from knowing with certainty that God's plan is still in effect and Jesus's sacrifice has changed the ending of our story.

Our hope can be found in our knowledge that God began His good work in the world and in us long ago, and He will finish it (Phil. 1:6). As John Piper said, "Hope comes from the promises of God rooted in the work of Christ."[5] Our hope should be built on nothing less than the promise that, through Jesus, our sins are forgiven and our future is secure.

> **Read 1 Peter 1:3–7. What does the living hope described in this passage look like in your life? How does hope in your inheritance change how you live today?**

In addition to God the Father and Christ the Son, we can also find our hope in the Holy Spirit. Paul's letter to the Romans lays out the gospel of Jesus Christ for his first-century readers and for us now. In today's verse from Romans 15:13, as Paul nears the end of his letter, he asks the Holy Spirit to fill believers with so much hope that it would overflow.

In John 14:25–27, Jesus promises His disciples that, though He would leave this earth, God the Father would send the Holy Spirit as a Comforter and Counselor. He promises that we will not be alone and that He leaves us with peace—the same peace Paul refers to in Romans 15:13. Though Paul expresses his desire that those who believe in Jesus would be so moved by the news of their salvation that their hearts would overflow with hope, he knew that we would need help.

When our hearts and minds fail us—despite our knowledge of and trust in God's Word and plans and our salvation through Christ—we can lean on the Holy Spirit to find hope. And if we will just ask, the Comforter and Counselor will create in us a heart of hope so abundant and resilient that it cannot be defeated by anything this world throws at us.

Reflect on today's reminders and truths about where we find our hope. Name one way you find hope in God the Father, in Jesus Christ, and in the Holy Spirit.

SCRIPTURE MEMORY MOMENT

Read Psalm 62:5–6 again. Consider texting the passage to a friend who might be encouraged by these words, and invite her to memorize it with you. Thank God for being our only and complete source of hope.

A PRAYER FOR TODAY

GOD, *thank You for being a source of abundant hope, my only true source. Thank You for manifesting hope through Your Word, Your plans for my life, Your faithfulness and love, salvation in Jesus, and the gift of the Holy Spirit. Open my eyes to all the places and ways You are giving me hope today. Amen.*

DAY 5

We have this hope as an anchor for the soul, firm and secure.

Hebrews 6:19

As we reach the end of the first week of this study, do you feel any more secure in your hope? What are some ways your ideas about hope have changed so far?

_____

_____

_____

_____

Have you ever washed a pair of shoes and then put them in the dryer? Or accidentally left change in your pocket when you put your pants in the wash? Something about hearing the banging of shoes or the clanging of nickels and dimes as they bounce around the drum of the dryer is so unsettling.

The jolt I feel when I hear that sound is what I think of when I imagine living without being tethered to a secure source of hope. Tossed about from one side to another, crashing into walls, being turned upside down and feeling helpless to get right side up again—it's the fate of tennis shoes in the dryer, and it's how I feel when I lose my grip on the hope God offers.

In Matthew Henry's commentary on the Bible, he describes Hebrews 6:19 like this:

> We are in this world as a ship at sea, liable to be tossed up and down, and in danger of being cast away. Our souls are the vessels. The comforts, expectations, graces, and happiness of our souls are the precious cargo with which these vessels are loaded. Heaven is the harbour to which we sail. The temptations, persecutions, and afflictions that we encounter are the winds and waves that threaten our shipwreck. We have need of an anchor to keep us sure and steady, or we are in continual danger.[6]

What might these metaphorical shipwrecks look like in your life? Hopelessness can lead to depression, addiction, broken relationships, and even poor health. When we panic at every provocation or slide into despair at every hurdle or disappointment, we are likely to hurt ourselves and those around us. We make unhealthy choices and get off the path God has placed us on, and we find it difficult or even impossible to do the good works He's created for us.

But we don't have to let our soul ships get blown off course and pushed around by the storm. As we've discussed this week, God is offering us hope and He *is* our hope. Because of God the Father, Jesus Christ, and the Holy Spirit, we have much to hope in and hope for. And when we do, we can endure today and take steps into tomorrow, confident that we can live well no matter what life brings.

What are some of the "shipwrecks" you've experienced in the past?

Our hope is an anchor that keeps us grounded when the world around us is constantly changing. So when change comes, we remember to turn away from what-ifs and worst-case scenarios and turn to the truth that God is with us through every twist and turn of this life. When the unexpected happens, when that middle-of-the-night phone call has the news we never imagined receiving, when the nightmare becomes reality, we can stand firm on the truth by praying and reading Scripture. We can be secure in God's love and in His Word, in His plans and His promises, and be comforted knowing those things never change.

In Psalm 112, the author writes about the traits of the righteous. Amid a long list of characteristics such as being gracious, generous, and compassionate, the psalmist says this about the righteous person: "He will never be shaken. . . . He will not fear bad news; his heart is confident, trusting in the LORD. His heart is assured; he will not fear" (vv. 6–8).

Think about the last time you waited for a test result or an important email. Did you have more in common with a ship without an anchor or with the righteous person described in this psalm? So many times, when we agonize over a decision or anxiously wait for someone else's verdict, we become the definition of *shaken* rather than assured, confident, or fearless.

Can you relate? Have you ever unraveled in the face of bad news or an abrupt change? Have you spent time waiting with white knuckles and gritted teeth rather than deep breaths and prayers of gratitude for what you trust God to do?

Imagine what it would be like to respond differently. What exactly does it mean to "have this hope as an anchor, firm and secure"?

> **Read Isaiah 26:3–4. What would it look and feel like to remain in perfect peace no matter how the world changes around you?**

Take time to reflect on the two passages we've studied this week. What are the results of hope described in Psalm 31:21–24 and Psalm 62:5–8?

The prophet Isaiah was tasked with warning the people of Israel to repent and return to God. He also had the honor of predicting the coming of Jesus. He describes Jesus as the cornerstone:

> So this is what the Sovereign Lord says:
>
> "See, I lay a stone in Zion, a tested stone,
>   a precious cornerstone for a sure foundation;
> the one who relies on it
>   will never be stricken with panic." (Isa. 28:16 NIV)

We can be secure in God's love and in His Word, in His plans and His promises, and be comforted knowing those things never change.

A cornerstone is the first stone laid for a building and the one all the other stones are built off of for a strong and steady foundation. That is what Jesus is for us—the cornerstone. This idea of Jesus being the crucial stone that anchors a structure, keeping everything stable and bearing the weight, is repeated throughout the Bible, from the psalms to the gospels and the letters of Paul. As our cornerstone, our anchor, our hope, the Lord gives us security and confidence that lead to courage and peace. And this is true and reliable no matter what our circumstances.

Over the next five weeks, we'll examine what the Bible says about finding hope when you're waiting, hurt, overwhelmed, or disappointed—and how that hope leads to peace, joy, and a deeper experience of God's love. My prayer is that by the end of our time in this study, your heart will be overflowing with hope.

Read 1 Corinthians 3:11. Write it in your own words and reflect on what it means in regard to your hope in God.

SCRIPTURE MEMORY MOMENT

Test yourself on Psalm 62:5–6. Try to write the passage or say it out loud from memory. As we move into the next week of our study, hide these words in your heart and reflect on them often. Perhaps write the verses on a sticky note and put it somewhere you'll see it every day.

A PRAYER FOR TODAY

GOD, *thank You for the gift of hope. Thank You for giving me a secure anchor that means I can have courage, strength, and peace even when the world is as chaotic as a dryer full of rocks. Help me hold tight to my hope. Help me hold tight to You. Amen.*

HOPE WHEN YOU'RE WAITING

Last week we began our exploration of what Scripture says about hope. We looked at where we place our hope and what we hope for, where our hope comes from, and the difference hope makes. This week, we're going to look at hope within a specific circumstance: waiting.

It's one thing to feel hopeful when all is going well and life is unfolding according to our own plans. But what happens when we don't get what we want right away—or ever? How do we continue believing that God is working on our behalf and that our future is secure when our circumstances are unfavorable and change seems out of reach? How do we hope while *waiting*?

In this week's opening story, Holley Gerth shares her story of hope. Pay attention to Holley's commitment to hope even when faced with repeated disappointments and to the incredible way God revealed His plans for her life. Take time to consider how God might be doing something similar in your own story as you answer today's reflection questions and read this week's memory verses.

A Story of Hope

The single pink line on the pregnancy test mocks me from the bathroom counter: *You'll never be a mother*. I drop it into the trash—along with my hope.

"God," I whisper, "why does this have to be so hard?"

That scenario repeated itself for almost a decade of my life. I know what it's like to wait for something that feels like it's never coming, to ugly cry, yell into your pillow, fight the urge to give up. Maybe you've been there too? Maybe you're there right now.

What I came to understand through that season is this: God can handle whatever we feel. The hard questions. The tough emotions. Our doubt and despair. Through it all, He's still there.

With the help of His relentless love, my heart began to slowly, unexpectedly heal. One night at our church small group, just after I'd had a miscarriage, I couldn't hold it together any longer. "I'm not okay," I told them. Instead of being dismissed for being too emotional or rebuked for not having enough faith, I experienced comfort and acceptance—and it felt like coming in from the cold.

God also began changing my perspective on motherhood. One morning I read the third chapter of Genesis, where Eve is called "the mother of all living." In that moment God seemed to whisper this truth to my heart: *All women are mothers. Because all women bring life to the world in some way.*

I realized I brought life into the world through my words. I birthed books. *I was a mother.*

Embracing that truth gave me new hope and helped fill the hollow space in my heart.

Years later I sat in my living room watching a documentary about kids who age out of the foster system. The narrator explained that when these children turn eighteen, they're often simply told, "You're on your own." The story touched me deeply, and when people asked if we'd considered adoption, I started answering, "If I adopt, I'll choose a twenty-year-old."

One time when I gave that response, a friend of mine asked, "Have you heard of Saving Grace?" It turned out that a transitional living home for foster girls aging out of the system was being started right there in my town. I connected with the founder, and when I told her my dream, she didn't look at me like I was crazy.

Life got busy and more years passed before I was invited to attend a banquet celebrating the accomplishments of the girls living at Saving Grace. God had impressed on my heart that my word for the next year of my life was *love*. And the night of the banquet I met my daughter: *Lovelle.*

How old was she? Twenty, of course. Lovelle and I had lunch together a few weeks later, and she asked me if I had kids. I gave her the short version, and before I left she said, "Well, you can just be my mom." She met my husband, Mark, and slowly, over many months of building trust, we became a family.

Fast-forward to a few days ago. My granddaughter Eula races around her backyard. The world is full of color this afternoon—yellow dandelions, the pink polka dots on her shirt, the blue sky above. She points out her favorite things to me. "Bird! Wagon! Dommi [the dog]!" When she finally pauses to catch her breath, I find myself in a state of wonder. *How did I end up in this moment?*

I think back to a decade of infertility for Mark and me, a lifetime of difficulty for our daughter, and how God brought us all together. I think of Lovelle's wedding day when she wore a white dress and danced with her dad. I think of being in the room when she gave birth, holding her hand and telling her again and again, "You are strong. You are brave. You can do this."

I think of the first time I held Eula, how she looked at me with her wide, curious eyes—the same ones staring at me now. Almost seven years have gone by since we met Lovelle, and it feels as if we've always been a family.

During my infertility, I struggled with thinking that God's timing must be off or that maybe circumstances in my life had somehow slipped out of His control. Maybe I wasn't good enough for Him to answer my prayers. I cried in the bathroom, shouted in frustration, found it hard to pray sometimes. Where was God? Why wasn't He doing what I wanted—and doing it *now*?

August 28 is the day we legally changed Lovelle's last name to ours. We call it "Gerth Day" and celebrate it every year like a birthday. And what day was Eula born? *August 28—Gerth Day.* When I held her for the first time, I knew deep in my soul that God's timing had never been off. He had always been in control, and He had better plans than all my demands.

I don't believe God caused my infertility. But I do believe that He is always working out His good plans for our lives, that there is so much more going on than what we can see with our eyes, that hope is a powerful thing and the desires of our heart will not go unmet—even if the answers to them look totally different than what we expect.

We all go through seasons of waiting. We can't determine what will happen next. But we can have hope because our story is not over. There's still so much I don't understand, but I know this: the Author is good, we are loved, and He alone holds the pen that gets to write "The End."

—HOLLEY GERTH

What is something you've been waiting for over a long period of time, something that has not happened yet?

_____

_____

_____

_____

Have you ever realized that God has answered your prayers in a significantly different way than you expected? What did you learn about God when you see the contrast between what He gave you and what you had planned for or wanted?

Read Jeremiah 29:11–13. This passage is part of a letter the prophet Jeremiah wrote to Israelites living in exile during the darkest time of their history. Verses 11–13 tell the exiles that God has a future for them that they could never imagine in that moment. Reading this today, we can be encouraged that God also has good plans for us. What does it look like for you to seek God with all your heart in the midst of waiting?

SCRIPTURE MEMORY MOMENT

This week's memory verses are Jeremiah 29:11–13. Write out the verses in your journal (from the NIV as printed here or from your favorite translation). Throughout the week, commit these words to memory as you ask God to create in you a heart of hope during times of waiting.

"For I know the plans I have for you," declares the LORD, "plans to prosper you and not to harm you, plans to give you hope and a future. Then you will call on me and come and pray to me, and I will listen to you. You will seek me and find me when you seek me with all your heart."

A PRAYER FOR TODAY

OH LORD, *I've been waiting so long. You know the desires of my heart, and You know how hard it is to keep waiting. Please be with me. Hear me. God, if You are already answering my prayers, please open my eyes to see Your hand at work in my life. And while I wait, create in me a heart full of hope in You, Your plans, and Your promises. Thank You, God, that my hope and future are secure in You. Amen.*

Deeply hurt, Hannah prayed to the LORD and wept with many tears. Making a vow, she pleaded, "LORD of Armies, if you will take notice of your servant's affliction, remember and not forget me, and give your servant a son, I will give him to the LORD all the days of his life, and his hair will never be cut."

While she continued praying in the LORD's presence, Eli watched her mouth. Hannah was praying silently, and though her lips were moving, her voice could not be heard. Eli thought she was drunk and said to her, "How long are you going to be drunk? Get rid of your wine!"

"No, my lord," Hannah replied. "I am a woman with a broken heart. I haven't had any wine or beer; I've been pouring out my heart before the LORD. Don't think of me as a wicked woman; I've been praying from the depth of my anguish and resentment."

Eli responded, "Go in peace, and may the God of Israel grant the request you've made of him."

1 Samuel 1:10–17

Think of a time when you were so distraught that you couldn't contain your grief. If another person was with you, how did they react to your pain? If you were alone in that moment, did you later share your grief with someone?

ER- 2001

Holley's story is particularly encouraging because we can see that God made sure she knew she wasn't alone in her sorrow, providing her with friends who offered her comfort when she was in pain. While the answers to her prayers that were eventually revealed are incredible, God didn't suddenly show up after years of neglect. In Holley's story—just like in Hannah's story in Scripture and in our own stories—we see that God was with her all along. Though He said, "Not yet," He also said, "You're not alone."

Throughout the Bible, God declares that He will never abandon us. Shortly before Moses dies, he tells the Israelites that God will never leave nor forsake them (Deut. 31:6)—the same thing God later reiterates to Joshua, their new leader. The Psalms are full of God's assurances that He will be with us at all times, and in his letter to the Romans, Paul goes into great detail of how certain we can be that we will never be separated from the love of God (Rom. 8:31–39).

While deeply comforting, God's promise to be near is offered not only to ease our pain or fear. The promise that we are not alone infuses our hearts with hope. Hope then empowers us to withstand painful situations and move forward into the future God has planned for us. Moses reminded Joshua and the Israelites that God would never leave them so that they might find the strength and courage to continue their journey to the promised land. After Hannah found solace in her prayers to

God's promise to be near is offered not only to ease our pain or fear. The promise that we are not alone infuses our hearts with hope.

God and reassurance in the kind words of Eli the priest, she was able to eat again and no longer felt despondent over her infertility (1 Sam. 1:17–18). And though Holley continued to be unable to get pregnant, God's love through her most painful season and the care she received from her community helped her heal and allowed her to be open to opportunities God placed in her path.

And that's the power of hope when we're waiting. It gives us not only the strength to endure challenges but also the strength to focus on God and the courage to step into the story that He's been writing for us all along.

> **In both Hannah's and Holley's situations, healing came after sharing their pain, even though their circumstances remained the same. If you've been waiting for an answer or a change, have you shared the depths of your struggle with anyone? Who could you turn to with transparency and honesty about your pain?**

One thing we need to note is that Hannah's hope was bolstered before she became pregnant. She trusted in the Lord even though her situation had not yet changed. She was still barren, was still being mocked by her husband's other wife, and had no guarantee that her life would ever look different—and yet after taking her burden to God, she walked away secure in her faith and hope. Similarly, in yesterday's story Holley shared that she never birthed a baby herself. But in the middle of her waiting for motherhood, God showed her other plans He had for her. Because she was focused on God and where He was guiding her, Holley was open to learning about kids aging out of the foster system, which led her to Lovelle, the young woman who would complete her family.

For both Holley and Hannah, their immediate situations didn't change. Their perspectives did. And God wants to offer that same powerful transformation to us.

When we remember that we are not alone, that God is with us in our pain and suffering, we find hope. When we focus on His love for us and His promise to someday work everything out for our good (Rom. 8:28), we find hope. When we place our hope in who God is—faithful, trustworthy, and kind—rather than just what He can do for us, then our present circumstances become less important. We might not stop hurting, but our hope becomes bigger than our pain and the causes of that pain. This hope is what allowed Paul to refer to his own troubles as "momentary light affliction" (2 Cor. 4:17), even though those very afflictions had overwhelmed him so completely that he "even despaired of life itself" (1:8). This hope is what makes all the difference in how we experience both the world and the Lord.

Read the following verses. How would believing in the unseen—both present and future—help you find hope while waiting?

- **Joshua 1:5, 9**
- **Isaiah 41:10, 13**
- **Hebrews 10:35–39**

Think of the part of your life where you have been waiting a long time for an answer or a change. If God does not answer your prayers in the way you want, if nothing ever changes in your external circumstances,

what truth can you still find hope in? (If you need help answering this question, Isaiah 43:1–13 is an excellent place to start.)

> ⟶ that God has plans
> for me and His will is always
> what's best

Because we live in a broken, imperfect world, most of us are waiting for something in every season of life. Infertility may not be your personal struggle, but God offers hope for all seasons of waiting—waiting for a job or for basic provision, waiting for a relationship to change, waiting for your health to improve. No matter your struggle, you aren't alone in feeling desperate, depressed, confused, or overwhelmed. And that means you aren't the only one who needs hope!

Though hope comes from God alone (remember last week's memory verses?), we can encourage one another the way Eli the priest eventually encouraged Hannah and the way Holley's friends encouraged her. We can be there for our friends with acceptance and kindness when they share their pain, and we can pave the way for God's hope to enter. In that way, the power of hope is exponential, multiplying as we point one another to the Lord and the promise that He is always with us.

Who do you know who's also waiting on God for something right now? How could you support this person and point them to the hope you're also finding during the wait?

SCRIPTURE MEMORY MOMENT

As you consider the power of hope while you're waiting, reflect again on Jeremiah 29:11–13. Write the passage three times in your journal, and ask God to help you hope in the truth that He is working out His plans for you even now.

A PRAYER FOR TODAY

GOD, *thank You for being with me while I wait, for hearing me and holding me close when I'm hurting. Please open my eyes to the foundational truths where I can find hope. Remind me of Your love and the work You're doing even when I can't see it. And if I can help someone else find their hope in You, Lord, please show me who and how. Thank You. Amen.*

God has given both his promise and his oath. These two
things are unchangeable because it is impossible for God to
lie. Therefore, we who have fled to him for refuge can have
great confidence as we hold to the hope that lies before us.
This hope is a strong and trustworthy anchor for our souls.

Hebrews 6:18–19 NLT

How do you feel when you read that it's impossible for God to lie? How does that statement affect your understanding of hope?

comforted, sure of God's integrity & character in all situations

Hannah isn't the only woman in the Bible who waited for years to have a baby. Abraham and Sarah waited for decades before finally becoming pregnant with their son, Isaac (Gen. 21:1–5). Like Hannah, Sarah felt so worn down by waiting that when she overheard God promising Abraham that she would one day bear a son, all she could do was laugh—possibly in wonder and delight at such a thought, but possibly in derision and doubt that it would ever happen.

Throughout their years of waiting, though, God kept Abraham's hope alive with repeated promises that He would bless Abraham with a large family. Read the following passages:

- Genesis 12:1–3
- Genesis 15:1–6
- Genesis 17:1–8

As you can see, God promised Abraham that He would make him (and his family) into a great nation, that his offspring would be as numerous as the stars, that he would be the fruitful father of many nations. And yet, Abraham was well into his seventies, his eighties, and even his nineties—so old that the writer of Hebrews tells us he was "as good as dead" (11:12). How could anyone hope for that long?

Abraham didn't have the advantage of God's written Word to consult for guidance and encouragement. He didn't have a long history of God's faithfulness to fall back on when he began to question God's plans for his life. But what Abraham did have that allowed him to confidently place his hope and build a strong foundation of faith was the actual, personal word of God. God spoke directly to him!

God told Abraham how important he was to God's plan and that he would bless Abraham if he would obey. God's promises gave Abraham all the hope he needed to wait decades before seeing his and Sarah's son born. And even when Abraham's faith wavered and he tried to force God's plan to fit into his and Sarah's timeline (see Gen. 16), God remained faithful to His promises.

Most of us today may not hear the audible voice of God, but we have the written Word of God that contains God's plans and promises as well as story after story of His faithfulness throughout the ages.

Read Jeremiah 29:11–13 again. How are God's promises in that passage, spoken to the Israelites through the prophet Jeremiah, similar to the words God spoke to Abraham?

promises for a rich future

Abraham lived in a polytheistic society, where people believed in and worshiped many gods, and yet he was able to recognize the one, true God. How have the beliefs of your family or community affected how you relate to and hope in God?

Just like biblical stories of God's faithfulness are a rich resource God uses to plant and nurture hope in our hearts, our own stories can achieve a similar effect. When we share with one another about the times when God has proved Himself faithful—the peace He gave in the hospital room, the comfort He provided when a prodigal child wandered, the unexpected answer that came on the verge of giving up—we remember together that placing our hope in God will never disappoint.

So many of the psalms show us how this is done. The psalmists joyfully share stories of God's love and faithfulness, how He created the world, rescued them from peril, and comforted them in distress. They rehearse these truths when faced with enormous challenges. The result?

Their hope is renewed and secure. Similarly, as today's passage from Hebrews points out, when we see that God's promises to Abraham were fulfilled, we can have confidence and find security by placing our hope in Him.

Psalm 145 is a helpful example of reflecting on God's character and behavior to create a heart of hope: "The LORD is gracious and compassionate, slow to anger and great in faithful love. The LORD is good to everyone; his compassion rests on all he has made" (vv. 8–9). The psalmist also goes into detail about all the amazing things God has done and how amazing He simply *is*, finishing with a hopeful declaration:

> My mouth will declare the LORD's praise;
> let every living thing
> bless his holy name forever and ever. (v. 21)

Turning to God's Word—and the stories of those who know God— leads to hope that is a strong and trustworthy anchor for our souls.

Do you have a story of God's faithfulness that you could share with someone? What's that story, who can you share it with, and how do you think that might increase your hope and theirs?

pregnancy

Yesterday we read the words God spoke to Joshua when he faced the challenge of leading the Israelites into the promised land after Moses's death. God promised Joshua both earthly success and the more important reward of His constant presence: "No one will be able to stand against you as long as you live. I will be with you, just as I was with Moses. I will not leave you or abandon you. Be strong and courageous, for you will distribute the land I swore to their ancestors to give them as an inheritance" (Josh. 1:5–6).

Toward the end of the book of Joshua, as his story is wrapping up, we read this summary:

> So the LORD gave Israel all the land he had sworn to give their ancestors, and they took possession of it and settled there. The LORD gave them rest on every side according to all he had sworn to their ancestors. None of their enemies were able to stand against them, for the LORD handed over all their enemies to them. None of the good promises the LORD had made to the house of Israel failed. Everything was fulfilled. (Josh. 21:43–45)

None of the Lord's promises failed. Everything happened that He said would happen. And that is how we know we can hope in Him. That is why our hope in Him is as secure and trustworthy as an anchor. Over and over throughout history and even in our own stories, we have seen God prove Himself trustworthy. So even when the wait seems to take longer than any person can stand, we can still hold on to hope in Him.

Start a list of promises God has kept. These can be promises you've seen God honor in your own life or in the lives of others, or they can be examples from the Bible. Make a list and put it in a place where you will see it and God can use it to help the hope in your heart grow.

SCRIPTURE MEMORY MOMENT

Memorizing Scripture is often called "hiding God's Word in our heart," and doing so helps us hold on to hope even when we're waiting. Take time today to recite Jeremiah 29:11–13 a few times as you write the passage in your journal, and ask God to hide His truth in your heart.

A PRAYER FOR TODAY

THANK YOU, GOD, *for the Bible. Thank You for ensuring that Your promises—and the way You keep them—were recorded over time. When I find it hard to hope, please remind me of the times You've kept promises to me, and help me hold on to the truth I've gained from Your Word. Thank You for being so unshakable that I can confidently hope in You. Amen.*

Dear brothers and sisters, be patient as you wait for the Lord's return. Consider the farmers who patiently wait for the rains in the fall and in the spring. They eagerly look for the valuable harvest to ripen. You, too, must be patient. Take courage, for the coming of the Lord is near.

James 5:7–8 NLT

When you find yourself waiting in a small, everyday way (perhaps in line at the store or for a doctor's appointment), what do you do to pass the time?

distraction - phone
people watch
chat with others

In the book of Matthew, we see Jesus telling several parables to illustrate truths about His Father's kingdom. In chapter 13, He describes a farmer who scatters seeds that land on various types of soil. Only the seed that falls on fertile soil ends up yielding a crop for the farmer, illustrating Jesus's point that not everyone who hears the Word of God will understand and believe it. However, it also provides encouragement for those of us who are waiting.

Because we have hope in what God is doing today and what He has planned for tomorrow, we can be obedient in how we wait.

God has promised a harvest (Gal. 6:9–10), an answer to our prayers, an end to our waiting. He hasn't told us when it will come, however, so we continue to wait. But in that wait, we shouldn't sit around and twiddle our thumbs. Instead, God urges us to continue planting seeds. Today's passage from James 5 tells the story of farmers who don't know when harvest will happen, but they faithfully plant and wait while looking forward to (or hoping for) that day.

While most of us probably are not actual farmers, we are called to plant seeds while we wait for the thing we are praying and hoping for. We plant seeds of health while we wait for a cure by getting enough rest, asking our doctor hard questions, and taking our vitamins or medication. We plant seeds of relationship while we wait for restoration or change by praying for, listening to, and serving our loved ones. We plant seeds of ministry while we wait for revival by praying for, serving, and sharing with our community. We place our hope in God, knowing He is faithful because we read it in His Word and we've seen it in our stories.

Think about the thing you're waiting for right now. What "seeds" could you plant while you hope in the Lord and trust in the future He's planned for you?

Have you witnessed or been the recipient of someone else's "seeds" (such as kindness, service, prayer) while they were in a season of waiting? How did their relentless hope while waiting affect your own journey of hope and faith?

Planting seeds (whether literally or figuratively) makes no sense if we have no hope for a future harvest. But because we have hope in what God is doing today and what He has planned for tomorrow, we can be obedient in how we wait. We see this in the biblical descriptions of farmers, and we see it in Holley's story when she invested her time writing and volunteering while still waiting to become a mother. We also see this in the context of this week's memory verses from Jeremiah.

One of the verses in the passage we're memorizing is quite popular in Christian circles. Many of us are quick to turn to or offer Jeremiah 29:11 as comfort when life isn't going according to our own expectations or plans. And while it is an encouragement for sure, that one verse is part of a much bigger picture:

> This is what the LORD of Armies, the God of Israel, says to all the exiles I deported from Jerusalem to Babylon: "Build houses and live in them. Plant gardens and eat their produce. Find wives for yourselves, and have sons and daughters. Find wives for your sons and give your daughters to men in marriage so that they may bear sons and daughters. Multiply there; do not decrease. Pursue the well-being of the city I have deported you to. Pray to the LORD on its behalf, for when it thrives, you will thrive."
>
> For this is what the LORD of Armies, the God of Israel, says: "Don't let your prophets who are among you and your diviners

> deceive you, and don't listen to the dreams you elicit from them, for they are prophesying falsely to you in my name. I have not sent them." This is the LORD's declaration.
>
> For this is what the LORD says: "When seventy years for Babylon are complete, I will attend to you and will confirm my promise concerning you to restore you to this place. For I know the plans I have for you"—this is the LORD's declaration—"plans for your well-being, not for disaster, to give you a future and a hope. You will call to me and come and pray to me, and I will listen to you. You will seek me and find me when you search for me with all your heart. I will be found by you"—this is the LORD's declaration—"and I will restore your fortunes and gather you from all the nations and places where I banished you"—this is the LORD's declaration. "I will restore you to the place from which I deported you." (Jer. 29:4-14)

What sticks out to you from this passage? What does God tell the Israelites to do while they wait to be rescued from exile?

Through the prophet Jeremiah, the Lord tells the Israelites to plant seeds while they wait on Him. He promises to rescue and restore them, but first He says they must make lives where they are—even though where they are is not where they want to be. He acknowledges that their difficult situation will last a long time, but He doesn't just shrug and say, "Well, hang in there!" He also doesn't let them off the hook for moving forward even when they feel stuck in a land that isn't their own. Instead, He tells them to pray and to plant, and He knows they can do it because of their hope in Him, His promises, and His plans.

Following God in obedience when you're in a season of waiting isn't easy, and God surely never indicates that He thinks it is. In fact, this just might be why we have so many psalms about how hard it is to wait but how helpful it is to hope anyway. If you're finding it hard to plant or produce or even pray while you wait, try reading Psalm 42.

In this psalm the author says, "I am deeply depressed; therefore I remember you" (Ps. 42:6). He knows that remembering the Lord will renew his hope. He also knows that hoping in God doesn't just mean crossing our fingers and wishing for a good outcome; it means standing firm in our faith, believing God has good plans for us (Jer. 29:11), and praising Him through the uncomfortable, messy in-between of waiting.

Even when our wait has gone on for decades, when we are disheartened and depressed, when it seems like the answer to our prayers may never come, we can still praise the One who never changes and is always with us. We can obey His commands to love others (aka "plant seeds"), and when we do, we can watch our hope grow deeper and stronger even while we continue to wait.

How can you nurture the growing hope in your heart today by remembering and praising God? (Note: If you are feeling "deeply depressed," as the psalmist says, we also encourage you to reach out to a trusted friend, pastor, or medical provider.)

SCRIPTURE MEMORY MOMENT

As we wait with expectation and hope, we can plant seeds of spiritual growth by memorizing God's Word. Write Jeremiah 29:11–13 on a sticky note and put it somewhere you'll see it often. Ask God to use these words to renew your hope.

A PRAYER FOR TODAY

GOD, *it's really hard to wait. You know there are places in my life where I don't want to be and circumstances that I long to be different. But I trust You and I'm placing my hope in You—for now and for always. Please show me what to do while I wait. Thank You for having a plan for me. Amen.*

Those who hope in the LORD
    will renew their strength.
They will soar on wings like eagles;
    they will run and not grow weary,
    they will walk and not be faint.
                    Isaiah 40:31 NIV

Think about a time when you waited for something longer than expected. What toll did that take on your health (physical, mental, emotional, spiritual, financial, or relational)?

_____

_____

_____

_____

One of the hardest parts of waiting can be the uncertainty. When we don't know how long a season will last, it can be challenging to handle the in-between, the unresolved, the when-will-this-ever-be-over nature of waiting. Our minds don't know how to prepare or protect us; our bodies remain in a state of fight-or-flight, unsure when relief will come; and budgeting our energy, our money, or our other resources is a nearly impossible math problem when we don't know all the factors.

In the book of Mark, we read about a woman who had been waiting for more than a decade. In her desperation and pain, she decided to approach Jesus, the famous healer.

> Now a woman suffering from bleeding for twelve years had endured much under many doctors. She had spent everything she had and was not helped at all. On the contrary, she became worse. Having heard about Jesus, she came up behind him in the crowd and touched his clothing. For she said, "If I just touch his clothes, I'll be made well." Instantly her flow of blood ceased, and she sensed in her body that she was healed of her affliction. (Mark 5:25–29)

Though you may not have been bleeding for the past twelve years, it's likely you've felt the exhaustion of a long season of waiting. Undiagnosed illness, chronic pain, a hurtful relationship, a rebellious child, overwhelming debt, even a disappointing career path—the difficulty of these struggles (and so many more) is multiplied by their indefinite duration. Not knowing how long the wait will last makes it harder. But hope! Hope is what we need at every point of the wait, whether we know exactly how long it will last or we go to bed each night unsure of what we'll face in the morning.

When we read about the bleeding woman, we can see that she had "endured much" and "spent everything she had," which points to her resilience in pursuing a solution. Even when her condition became worse, still she persevered. Clearly she had hope that she would be healed, that her situation would not last forever. And then when she heard about Jesus, the Messiah who was traveling to teach and heal, she finally had something more substantial to hope in and to hope for. She believed so strongly—hoped so firmly—in Jesus and what He could do that she was healed just by touching the edge of His clothing.

Read Mark 5:25–34. Remember back to week 1 of this study and how we discussed John Piper's definition of hope as "faith in future tense." Beyond physical healing, what do you think the woman in this story was hoping for? Do you think it happened in the way she expected?

While we don't know all the details of this woman's pain or the consequences she faced as a result, we can safely assume they were bad. Her hope, like we read about in today's Scripture from Isaiah 40:31, gave her renewed strength to endure and persevere. What do you need strength to endure today?

Though we all face seasons of waiting, hope makes a difference in how we experience the wait. Peter, one of Jesus's disciples, wrote a letter to teach believers about God's grace that helps us bear suffering in this world. Toward the end of the letter, he says, "In his kindness God called you to share in his eternal glory by means of Christ Jesus. So after you have suffered a little while, he will restore, support, and strengthen you, and he will place you on a firm foundation" (1 Pet. 5:10 NLT).

And that's the difference right there! Our strength may be sapped by the waiting, but it will be renewed when we place our hope in God and persevere in step with His plans. Not only does God promise to never leave us (Heb. 13:5), but He also promises to restore us, support us, and yes, strengthen us. So we are able to try again and pursue another answer and even accept our current circumstances—whether that's chronic illness like the bleeding woman in Mark 5, unemployment, difficult relationships, mental health challenges, or something else. In the meantime, then, we wait for the change we know will come eventually. Because we have hope in the Lord, we know we can give Him our every burden (Matt. 11:28–30) and He will in return give us peace and strength.

> **What would it look like to hand over the burden of your waiting to the Lord, to have such hope—in what He's doing now and what He will do in the future—that you allow Him to restore, support, and strengthen you? What is standing in the way of that kind of hope?**

As we've already discovered, the psalms are full of songs written by people who were waiting. In Psalm 40 we see the difference hope makes when David writes about how God rescued him, leading David to praise Him and share his story so others can also find hope in God.

> I waited patiently for the Lord to help me,
>   and he turned to me and heard my cry.
> He lifted me out of the pit of despair,
>   out of the mud and the mire.
> He set my feet on solid ground
>   and steadied me as I walked along.

> He has given me a new song to sing,
>   a hymn of praise to our God.
> Many will see what he has done and be amazed.
>   They will put their trust in the LORD. (Ps. 40:1–3 NLT)

See, while God is compassionate toward us, caring about our pain and struggles, He has a greater purpose for works He is doing in our lives. When He renews our strength, we're then able to help others find hope by telling our story. David asked God for wisdom and understanding while he was waiting (Ps. 25:4–5), so while he was waiting and hoping, he was also learning about the Lord. Then, when his wait was finally over, he was already praising God and showing others how hope could change their lives too.

What have you learned about God while waiting? Have you shared that with anyone? If not, who could you share your story with soon?

_____

_____

_____

_____

_____

Not only does God promise to never leave us, but He also promises to restore us, support us, and yes, strengthen us

SCRIPTURE MEMORY MOMENT

Test yourself on Jeremiah 29:11–13. Have you committed it to memory? As we move on to the next week of our study, continue to reflect on these words and the hope you find in God's promises and plans.

A PRAYER FOR TODAY

DEAR GOD, *thank You for everything You're doing in my heart while I wait. Thank You for being the ever-loving, never-changing foundation I can put my hope in, no matter how long this season lasts. Please give me peace while I wait, the strength to endure, and the opportunity to share with others everything You've done in my life. Thank You, God. Amen.*

HOPE
WHEN YOU'RE
HURT

Last week we looked at how hope can make a difference when we're in a season of waiting. This week we're going to examine what Scripture says about finding hope when we've been hurt. Though everything God created is good (1 Tim. 4:4), sin has warped this world, creating a cycle of brokenness capable of inflicting deep pain. Through it all, though, He promises to never leave our side and to redeem every injury and ache in the end. And in that, we can find hope that sustains us through the darkest valleys.

Today's story of hope comes at great cost. One of our dear (in)courage writers is bravely sharing her story of sexual assault. As you read Aliza's story of trauma, don't miss the thread of hope that winds through it, guiding our sister in Christ—and us—right back to the One who heals the brokenhearted.

A Story of Hope

I couldn't stop trembling.

It had been two years, but my body quivered with the weight of it. I was walking down the street from the Canadian newsroom where I worked to my car parked a couple of blocks away. I stood still, waiting for the traffic light to change, but inside I was shaking.

I could feel it all over again: the trauma taking place in my body. It didn't matter that I was in the middle of a busy city—I felt like I had on the day it happened. I was hot and cold all at once.

Will I ever get past this, God? Tears threatened to fall, but I saw the light change, indicating my turn to cross the road. I wiped my face with the back of my hand, crossed the street, and got into my car. It took me a couple of extra seconds to get my keys into the ignition. I felt nauseous and jumpy. I took a deep breath and drove home.

This has happened a few times. I never know when it's coming—if I'll be triggered by a comment or a news article or nothing specific at all. I could be driving in my car or sitting on my couch at home when I suddenly feel the trauma replay in my mind and body.

I was twenty-two years old when my first boyfriend sexually assaulted me, though at the time I didn't know those were the words to describe what had happened.

He was the first boy to ever kiss me, the first to ever hold my hand. I didn't know what love or desire could feel like. He was older—and I thought wiser—than I was. He read Christian books about marriage and told me that if we got married he'd make me a home studio so I could paint.

I wanted to be loved so badly.

After I grasped what had happened, I didn't know how to talk about it. I broke up with him two days after the assault when he again told me he wanted to marry me and—like a veil being torn from my face, allowing my eyes to truly see—I realized for the first time that I didn't want to spend my life with him.

For months I didn't tell anyone. I numbed my grief with hundreds of hours of television. I felt like a shell of who I once was—as if all the joy and tenacity and sparkle God had lovingly crafted within me had been scooped out each time my boyfriend touched me when I told him no.

About six months after the assault, I preached at an event for high schoolers and told them about what had happened. I was desperate for someone to hear me and affirm that the pain clawing me open wasn't going to kill me. Yet telling a roomful of strangers wasn't wise; those girls could not properly hold the pain I hadn't yet sorted through my-self, and I shouldn't have expected them to.

Every time I told someone—whether it was that group of high school girls or any of my friends—I just felt more alone. I needed someone to tell me it wasn't my fault, that I wasn't dirty or stained. But no one knew what to say.

My shame over the assault seemed to carve itself into me, leaving me feeling cold and ripped open. I cried myself to sleep at night. I did not know how to trust God. I called a sexual assault hotline and spoke to a counselor. I spoke to a Christian counselor after that, and then later to another one. I read books on healing after sexual assault.

On a summer evening a few weeks after I'd felt the trauma replay its way through my body as I walked to my car from work, I told my friend Michelle.

She asked me if I was okay. I told the truth and said, "No." I told her everything. It was the middle of summer, but I was freezing. My body couldn't stop shaking. I shared the story in haphazard pieces, my tears and sobs interrupting me. My friend stayed quiet, listening, creating space for me to tell her whatever I wanted to.

When I turned to her after I was finished, I saw she was crying too. I could hardly believe that someone would cry with me.

She told me it wasn't my fault. She told me she was sorry. She told me there was nothing wrong with me. She told me I didn't ask for it. She told me God was with me—even when it felt like I was alone.

I felt something new form inside my heart that night as Michelle's words started to heal me: I felt hope.

The hope was ever so small, hardly big enough to hold in the palm of my hand, but it was still there. For the first time in a long time, I had hope that maybe I'd be okay.

I had hope that this wouldn't be the defining moment of my life.

I had hope that I could someday trust a good man and that I could get married and wouldn't be hurt this way by him.

I had hope that Jesus had not left me, not even in my darkest valley, but had actually been beside me all along.

I had hope that instead of remaining steeped in darkness and unforgiveness, I could choose to leave my shame behind me and step into the light.

It was small, but still, it was hope.

—ALIZA LATTA

Have you ever been hurt so badly that you didn't know how to talk about it? Take a moment to reflect on that situation and describe it here if you can.

Think about a time (or times) when you've been physically or emotionally wounded. How did that experience affect your view of God?

Psalm 23:4 talks about the gift of choosing to hope while walking through a dark valley. The psalmist David describes peace and an absence of fear because he knows God is with him in that dark place. Read Psalm 23 and then write what stands out to you about God's presence and/or reflect on the impact of God's presence through your own personal valley.

_____

_____

_____

_____

SCRIPTURE MEMORY MOMENT

This week's memory verse is Psalm 23:4. Write the verse in your journal from the translation of your choice (CSB is printed here). Throughout the week, commit these words to memory as you ask God to create in you a heart of hope when you're hurt.

Even when I go through the darkest valley,
I fear no danger,
for you are with me;
your rod and your staff—they comfort me.

A PRAYER FOR TODAY

HEAVENLY FATHER, *thank You for never leaving my side when I go through even the darkest valleys. I know it's likely I'll hurt and grieve again. When I do, I ask that You walk with me and give me comfort and strength to process the pain and move forward. May Your love redeem my past, heal my present, and guide my future. My hope is in You. Amen.*

Even when I go through the darkest valley,
I fear no danger,
for you are with me;
your rod and your staff—they comfort me.

Psalm 23:4

Like many of the psalms, Psalm 23 uses figurative language to describe the author's experience. What does "the darkest valley" mean to you? What situations does it bring to mind?

Before he was a king, the psalmist David was a shepherd, and in Psalm 23 he uses metaphors that would have been familiar to those living and working in the ancient Near Eastern world. Wadis are riverbeds that are usually dry, and they form deep valleys that shepherds must often cross when moving their flocks. In the CSB translation, verse 4 refers to "the darkest valley," but other translations call it "the valley of the shadow of death." According to the NIV Application Commentary, the Hebrew words used in the original text mean "shadow" and "death," and when put together in this way, they communicate "the shadowiest of all shadows."[1] While we may not have a working knowledge of Middle Eastern topography, anyone who's been in a (literally) dark space can understand shadowy shadows. And anyone who's gone through something incredibly painful—whether that's assault like Aliza experienced or abandonment, abuse, or betrayal—resonates with the word picture of a dark valley.

This week we're only memorizing the fourth verse of this psalm, but reading the chapter in its entirety is a must if we're going to glean a full understanding of the hope that can be found even in those dark shadows and deep valleys. Let's do that right now.

> The LORD is my shepherd;
> I have what I need.
> He lets me lie down in green pastures;
> he leads me beside quiet waters.
> He renews my life;
> he leads me along the right paths
> for his name's sake.
> Even when I go through the darkest valley,
> I fear no danger,
> for you are with me;
> your rod and your staff—they comfort me.
> You prepare a table before me
> in the presence of my enemies;
> you anoint my head with oil;
> my cup overflows.
> Only goodness and faithful love will pursue me
> all the days of my life,
> and I will dwell in the house of the LORD
> as long as I live. (Ps. 23:1–6)

In this short chapter of the Bible, we can see several themes that we've already covered in the first two weeks of this study. David writes about God's provision (v. 1) and finding rest, renewal, and guidance in Him (vv. 2–3). Further, he praises and thanks God for protection and salvation (vv. 5–6). As we've discussed, all of these gifts are reasons we place our hope in the Lord.

Think of a dark valley you've walked through or a shadow currently hanging over you. Which attributes of God have brought you comfort? (Note: Your answer may include characteristics mentioned in the previous paragraph, or it may include others. It's also okay if you haven't been able to find hope or comfort in the Lord before now. If that's the case, reflect on that experience here.)

Read Lamentations 3:19–26. In the New Living Translation, verses 20–21 say, "I will never forget this awful time, as I grieve over my loss. Yet I still dare to hope." Do you think it's possible to hope in the Lord and His faithful love when you're still hurt and even bitter? Why or why not?

These verses in Lamentations are a bright spot in the middle of a dark book that expresses great sorrow. The prophet Jeremiah wrote this lament shortly after the fall of Jerusalem in 586 BC. The Israelites had been carried away into captivity and exile in Babylon, where they would remain for seventy years. To say Jeremiah was grieved by the plight of his people would be an understatement. He was devastated, and he didn't hesitate to say so. The earlier verses of Lamentations 3 will give you a clearer picture of just how much he was hurting. Even the verse immediately before he begins to hope again says, "Everything I had hoped for from the LORD is lost!" (Lam. 3:18 NLT).

Jeremiah's desperate words illustrate that even though he had placed his hope in the Lord (and encouraged his people to do the same), he also fell into the trap of hoping in the outcomes he was asking for and expecting. However, beginning in verse 21, Jeremiah is purposeful to remember that no matter what his circumstances are, no matter how God has answered his prayers, God's love and compassion never end— and therefore his hope is secure!

Perhaps you've fallen into the same trap as Jeremiah, trying to trust God but also placing your hope in the results you desire. Perhaps you believe God can sustain you in your darkest days and will work on your behalf for a brighter future, but your idea of that bright future doesn't necessarily match His. If that's the case, you may find yourself lamenting like Jeremiah if you don't get the job, healing doesn't happen, your relationship isn't reconciled, your loved ones aren't kept safe, or any number of painful things happens.

> **The original Hebrew word for the title of Lamentations can be translated as "Alas!" If you were to write your own laments (perhaps beginning with "Alas!"), what would you say? Express any sorrow you hold and write a few laments here, but end with a reminder of true hope like Jeremiah does. Read Lamentations 3:22–26, 31–33, and 55–58 for ideas.**

Like Jeremiah, Job experienced deep grief in a dark valley but still managed to hold on to his eternal, foundational hope in the Lord. Job was a good man whom God allowed Satan to test. Though he had been healthy and wealthy and had a large family, Job lost it all. He became very sick, his children died, and all his livestock were stolen or killed. Job's wife told him to curse God and die, and his friends (who initially showed up to support him) repeatedly questioned and doubted his integrity since God was allowing such devastation in his life.

Now, that's not to say that Job took this incredibly painful season calmly or happily. Oh no. He goes around and around with God, asking Him for healing and eventually begging God to let him die. And rather than demonstrating His compassion in the way Job was expecting, God responds by reminding Job that He is in charge! (See Job 38–41.) But even then, Job trusts in God's sovereignty. Job rebukes his friends, saying, "God might kill me, but I have no other hope. I am going to argue my case with him. But this is what will save me—I am not godless. If I were, I could not stand before him" (Job 13:15–16 NLT).

Even when God chose to allow the absolute worst to happen in his life, Job was determined to trust God anyway. Likewise, after taking all his pain to the Lord, Jeremiah chose to continue hoping in God and His faithful love. We saw this same determined hope in Aliza's story. After a time of mourning and processing, she was again able to grasp the hope she has in God's love and His good plans for her life. In all three of these examples, the person experiencing pain trusted that the eternal glory coming would far outweigh their "momentary light afflictions," like Paul wrote about in 2 Corinthians and like we discussed earlier in this study.

In week 1 we studied 2 Corinthians 4:16–18. Just after those verses, Paul goes on to say, "For we know that if our earthly tent we live in is destroyed, we have a building from God, an eternal dwelling in the heavens, not made with hands" (5:1). Clearly, our eternal hope in God's plans and in the work of Jesus Christ is what makes the pain of this world bearable and keeps us grounded in hope even when our hearts or bodies might writhe in pain.

> If your "earthly tent" is destroyed—or if you are caused great pain—how will your knowledge of salvation affect how you respond? If you're currently experiencing this kind of sorrow, invite the Lord into that pain. Ask Him to remind you of His love and to renew your spirit (2 Cor. 5:17).

_____

_____

_____

_____

SCRIPTURE MEMORY MOMENT

Scripture makes it clear that we will experience pain in this life. Committing to memory words that remind you to hope in God—such as this week's memory verse from Psalm 23:4—will prepare you for those seasons. Write this week's verse in your journal three times.

A PRAYER FOR TODAY

OH LORD, *I'm so glad to know that even when life is dark and painful, You are here with me. Thank You for staying with me and loving me faithfully. When this world hurts me, God, show me that You're still here with me. Show me how to keep trusting You and Your plan for my life. Help me through the valley. Amen.*

The LORD is close to the brokenhearted
and saves those who are crushed in spirit.

Psalm 34:18 NIV

Think of a time when you've been brokenhearted. How did God show you He was with you? If you didn't feel God's presence during that time, reflect on that instead.

In the story Aliza shared with us, it's clear that in addition to the physical injury she suffered, she was deeply affected emotionally. Being horribly abused by someone she trusted understandably broke her heart. As she dealt with the aftermath of that incident, Aliza felt alone in her pain and shame until her friend reminded her that, while God certainly did not cause the assault, He was with her when it happened and He continued to be with her in every sad, scared, confused moment afterward.

The thing that has caused you pain may look completely different from Aliza's experience. But today's verse offers a foundational truth that can keep us all from becoming hopeless: "The LORD is close to the brokenhearted" (Ps. 34:18 NIV).

Psalm 34 was written by David after the Lord had rescued him once again from the murderous King Saul (1 Sam. 21:10–22:1). David writes words of praise, thanking God for hearing and answering his cry for help:

> I sought the LORD, and he answered me;
>   he delivered me from all my fears.
> Those who look to him are radiant;
>   their faces are never covered with shame.
> This poor man called, and the LORD heard him;
>   he saved him out of all his troubles. (Ps. 34:4–6 NIV)

Clearly, David is overjoyed by his rescue and is motivated to share his story with others. As we read more of this chapter, though, we should define a few terms David uses in order to better understand the message God has for us here.

Read Psalm 34:17–20. David tells us that God will deliver the righteous "from all their troubles." That sounds like a guarantee that if we're righteous, God will fix all of our problems. Could that be right? Not quite.

Reading that the Lord hears "the righteous" might feel discouraging to you if you assume you can't possibly be righteous—that is, free from sin and guilt. After all, as we read in Romans 3:10–12 (echoing Psalms 14 and 53), "There is no one righteous, not even one." Fortunately, that's not the end of the story. While we cannot be blameless or even good enough to be called righteous on our own, Jesus makes us righteous. Through His death and resurrection, He paid the penalty for our sins to make us right with God.

Have you accepted the gift of righteousness and salvation that Jesus is offering to you? Have you believed in Him, asked Him to forgive you,

and committed to following Him? If you have, journal here about the difference that's made in your life. If you have not, write about what's holding you back.

_____

_____

_____

_____

Returning to today's Scripture, we've answered what makes a person righteous—that is, right in the eyes of God. Does following Jesus mean that all our problems will be eliminated? Of course not. In John 16:33 (NIV), Jesus says, "In this world you will have trouble. But take heart! I have overcome the world." (Other Bible versions translate "trouble" as "suffering," "tribulation," or "trials and sorrows.") Jesus isn't preparing His followers for a possible contingency. No, He's saying we will certainly face challenges and hardships in this world. But He also says, "Take heart!" and that is where the promises of Psalm 34 come in.

David isn't promising that God will wave a magic wand and solve every problem we face. Instead, he's pointing us to the hope we have in a loving Father. While God never promises to prevent every problem, He vows to walk through trials with us, to give us comfort and strength to endure the darkest valleys, and ultimately to deliver us from a life and an eternity without Him. God delivers us from our troubles through Jesus Christ.

> Therefore, since we have been made right in God's sight by faith, we have peace with God because of what Jesus Christ our Lord has done for us. Because of our faith, Christ has brought us into this place of undeserved privilege where we now stand, and we confidently and joyfully look forward to sharing God's glory. (Rom. 5:1–2 NLT)

When you read Psalm 34 through the lens of eternal rescue rather than an immediate solution to your problems, how does that make you feel?

Read Psalm 34:18 again. When you are crushed or brokenhearted, what difference does it make knowing that God's presence is available to you and that He promises to be with you when you're hurting?

Not only does God promise to be with us when we are in pain, but He also knows deep sorrow Himself. Read Mark 14:34–36. Jesus had just eaten His last meal with the disciples, where He announced that one of them would betray Him and that Peter would deny Him. After supper, Jesus and eleven of the disciples went out to a place called Gethsemane. Jesus then took His closest friends—Peter, James, and John—apart from the others and asked them to keep watch while He prayed. This is what He told them before leaving to pray (from four different English translations):

- "I am deeply grieved to the point of death." (CSB)
- "My soul is overwhelmed with sorrow to the point of death." (NIV)

- "My soul is exceedingly sorrowful, even to death." (NKJV)
- "My soul is crushed with grief to the point of death." (NLT)

Even though Jesus was fully God, He also was fully man. And the weight of what He was going to do on the cross—and the inevitable betrayal by those He loved so deeply—was crushing. Finding His friends asleep after He'd asked them to stay awake and keep watch with Him in His grief must have multiplied Jesus's pain. Just like Aliza, who longed for a friend to talk to about her painful experience, and like the psalmists, who begged God not to abandon them (e.g., Pss. 13 and 22), Jesus did not want to be alone in His sorrow.

The feelings of abandonment and isolation, the confusion about why God has allowed the thing that's hurt us, and the fear that God has left us alone in this world multiply our pain. But the knowledge that God is actually with us in every season, that He will never leave us, and that He specifically cares for the brokenhearted divides and lessens our pain in even the most horrible circumstances. Our hope in God to be with us and, as we discussed in week 2, our confidence in His good plan for our life lessen the sting of sorrow while we're still in that dark valley.

Romans 8:38–39 says that nothing can separate us from the love of God. Have you ever thought that your situation was too ugly, too messy, too painful for God to stick by you? Or that your circumstances were just too much for God to overcome? How did you feel in that season? How do you feel now as you consider His many promises to never leave you or be separated from you?

Imagine God is physically sitting right next to you. What would you say to Him right now? What would you ask Him?

_____

_____

_____

_____

SCRIPTURE MEMORY MOMENT

We know God is with us because of the promises in Scripture. Memorizing those words will help us stay hopeful even when life is most painful. Write Psalm 23:4 in your journal and take time to read it aloud several times as you work on committing God's promise to memory.

A PRAYER FOR TODAY

JESUS, *I'm so grateful You understand how I feel when I'm hurting and alone. Thank You for Your promises to never leave me and to heal my broken heart. Thank You for the sacrifices You made so that I can be righteous in God's eyes and therefore be in relationship with You. Please make me aware of Your presence when I'm hurting. Amen.*

Now is your time of grief, but I will see you again and you will rejoice, and no one will take away your joy.

John 16:22 NIV

What is something about heaven that you're looking forward to?

In the first week of this study, we discussed Paul's second letter to the church in Corinth encouraging them to persevere through difficult times. He said, "Therefore we do not give up. Even though our outer person is being destroyed, our inner person is being renewed day by day. For our momentary light affliction is producing for us an absolutely incomparable eternal weight of glory. So we do not focus on what is seen, but on what is unseen. For what is seen is temporary, but what is unseen is eternal" (2 Cor. 4:16–18). In other words, life is hard now, but those trials will seem small compared to the eternal joy of our eternal salvation in Christ.

Long before Paul penned his letters, Jesus had said similar words to the disciples in the days leading up to His crucifixion. In John 14:1–4, He intentionally encourages them to not be troubled but to take comfort in the knowledge that He's going to prepare a place for them in heaven. Later, in John 16:22, He acknowledges that they will grieve when He leaves them, but He promises to see them again—and that His return will bring them everlasting joy.

Over and over again, we're seeing this truth: Life is hard now, but it won't always be that way. Our hope is in God because He is the one who will bring us salvation and joy that never ends.

How does trusting that joy is in your future change your perspective on today?

Holding tight to hope in the eternal joy God promises us can be difficult when we're still suffering. It can be even harder when we find ourselves hung up on anger, blame, and bitterness. Whether or not your pain was physical abuse like Aliza endured, you may be tempted to seek out a person to blame for your pain. The spouse who filed for divorce, the parent who spoke cruel words to you, the driver who caused the accident, the bank who raised your interest rate or gave your account to a collector, the doctor who prescribed the addictive drug—anyone who's caused us pain can make an appealing target for all our anguish.

But if we focus all our energy on blaming the people we believe are responsible for our pain, we won't be able to receive the comfort, the hope, and the joy God wants to give us. In Matthew 6:19–24, Jesus talks about money and materialism, but the overarching principle of His teaching applies here. In verse 21, He says that where we place our treasure (which could include our attention, our energy, our time) indicates what we value most. He then goes on to say, "No one can serve two masters, since either he will hate one and love the other, or he will be devoted to one and despise the other. You cannot serve both God and money" (v. 24).

> **Read Matthew 6:19–24. Where are you placing your treasure (your attention, energy, or time) right now? Is that consistent with what you truly value most?**

> **If you imagine God as a "master" and your pain (or its cause) as a second "master," which master are you serving? What would it look like to invest your treasure and your service completely in God?**

Our hope is in God because He is the one who will bring us salvation and joy that never ends.

Hagar is an example of a woman who knew all too well how it feels to suffer because of others' choices. In week 2 we looked at the story of Abraham and Sarah (originally called Abram and Sarai before God changed their names in Genesis 17), learning about how they held on to hope for a child even when God's promise took decades to be fulfilled. Abram's faith was enormous and enduring. His hope was firmly placed in the Lord. However, he was far from perfect, and at one point during his and Sarai's long wait for a child, they decided to take matters into their own hands.

In an attempt to fulfill God's promise on his own, Abram slept with Sarai's servant, Hagar, who became pregnant. Though the scheme had been Sarai's idea to begin with, she treated Hagar so badly during the pregnancy that Hagar ran away. An angel of the Lord came to Hagar and urged her to return to her mistress. The angel said that Hagar would give birth to a son, which was greatly valued in that culture, and that God would give her more descendants than she could count (Gen. 16:10–11). Though her problems certainly didn't end at that time, Hagar was given hope in what God was doing in her life. In addition, she was encouraged because God saw her in her suffering and didn't abandon her.

Read Genesis 16:13 (in the New Living Translation, if possible). What does Hagar call God, and why? What do you need God to see in your life? What difference would that make for you?

Later, after Sarah finally became pregnant and gave birth to Isaac, Hagar's son, Ishmael, did not get along with Isaac. At Sarah's urging and with God's permission, Abraham sent Hagar and Ishmael away. With no way to provide for herself or her son, Hagar sat down and sobbed, certain that her son would die there in the desert (Gen. 21:9–16). But once again, God was with her. An angel of the Lord came and told her that Ishmael's descendants would become a great nation, and the angel showed her a well of water so they could survive. Yes, Hagar had been badly treated and abandoned by Abraham, but God was with her and Ishmael, and He provided for them.

No matter who or what has hurt you, God will be with you and will provide for you too.

> **God didn't remove the difficulties from Hagar's life, but He gave her hope by assuring her that He saw her and that He was making a way for her to move forward into the rest of her life and leave Abraham and Sarah behind. What would it look like for you to move forward from who or what has hurt you?**

SCRIPTURE MEMORY MOMENT

The rod and staff mentioned in Psalm 23:4 are tools a shepherd would have used for stability and to protect the sheep. Today, practice reading the verse out loud as you imagine having the instruments of God's guidance and protection while walking through a dark valley.

A PRAYER FOR TODAY

DEAR GOD, *thank You for saving me and for the joy You promise is coming. While I'm still hurting, though, it's hard to focus on that and on You! Please help me remember what I value most, Lord, and where my hope truly lies. Please help me move past the pain into Your arms and the future You're planning for me. Amen.*

Blessed be the God and Father of our Lord Jesus Christ, the Father of mercies and the God of all comfort. He comforts us in all our affliction, so that we may be able to comfort those who are in any kind of affliction, through the comfort we ourselves receive from God. For just as the sufferings of Christ overflow to us, so also through Christ our comfort overflows. If we are afflicted, it is for your comfort and salvation. If we are comforted, it is for your comfort, which produces in you patient endurance of the same sufferings that we suffer. And our hope for you is firm, because we know that as you share in the sufferings, so you will also share in the comfort.

2 Corinthians 1:3–7

Who has comforted you during painful seasons?

_____

_____

_____

_____

Paul's first letter to the believers in Corinth focused largely on working together, worshiping together, and loving one another. His second letter to the Corinthians speaks more to individual faith, specifically teaching about the way God gives us strength when we're weak. Paul begins this letter with praise to God for comforting him in his own afflictions, which has allowed him to comfort others.

Paul's afflictions (also translated as "troubles," "tribulations," "trials," or "oppression") were great. As a result of his ministry and testimony about Jesus Christ as the Son of God, he had been beaten with rods, stoned, and imprisoned. During his travels he was often hungry and cold, and he had been shipwrecked three times! (For the full list of the hardships Paul endured, read 2 Cor. 11:24–28.) And yet we read here that Paul was thankful for these incredibly hard times because they were opportunities for God to work in his life and provide him comfort—so much comfort that it naturally overflowed to others he met who were also suffering.

The Message puts it this way: "All praise to the God and Father of our Master, Jesus the Messiah! Father of all mercy! God of all healing counsel! He comes alongside us when we go through hard times, and before you know it, he brings us alongside someone else who is going through hard times so that we can be there for that person just as God was there for us" (2 Cor. 1:3–4). God loves us deeply and does not delight in our suffering. But when we do suffer because of living in a broken world, He is with us. And His presence is a double gift, offering us both comfort and purpose. Even in the most painful circumstances, we have hope to endure today and to trust the future He's planning for us.

While you may not have been beaten, stoned, imprisoned, or shipwrecked, you've probably experienced hard times during your life. Nobody looks forward to the death of loved ones, divorce, debt, depression, or any other affliction we may suffer, yet God promises to comfort

God loves us deeply and does not delight in our suffering. But when we do suffer because of living in a broken world, He is with us.

us—and to such an extent that we are then equipped and compelled to comfort others.

Have you seen this happen in your own life? How have you been able to comfort someone after experiencing a similar painful situation?

In the Old Testament book of Ruth, we find the story of Ruth and Naomi. They experienced great affliction but also demonstrated great compassion to each other in their shared experiences. Naomi and her husband had left their home in Judah during a famine and raised their two sons in a land called Moab. Naomi's husband died, and later, after marrying local Moabite women, her two sons also died. Naomi and her two daughters-in-law, Ruth and Orpah, were left alone.

Naomi decided to return to her people in Judah, and when her daughters-in-law began traveling with her, she urged them to go back to their own families rather than embarking on a long journey to an unfamiliar place. She thanked them for their kindness and wished them well, and when they resisted leaving her, she pointed out that she had nothing to offer them.

> But Naomi replied, "Return home, my daughters. Why do you want to go with me? Am I able to have any more sons who could become your husbands? Return home, my daughters. Go on, for I am too old to have another husband. Even if I thought there was still hope for me to have a husband tonight and to bear sons, would you be willing to wait for them to grow up? Would you restrain yourselves from remarrying? No, my

> daughters, my life is much too bitter for you to share, because the Lord's hand has turned against me." (Ruth 1:11–13)

Naomi was bitter about the turns her life had taken, and at that point she believed that God had abandoned her in her pain. But He had not. Given what we know about God's character, we must not presume He caused Ruth and Orpah to be widowed simply so they would understand their mother-in-law's pain. Still, it's evident that part of His care for Naomi involved putting her in relationship with other women who were going through the same kind of grief that she was. Though Orpah reluctantly obeyed when Naomi insisted that she return to her own family, Ruth was a bit more stubborn. Determined to support her mother-in-law and show her compassion in their shared grief, Ruth refused to leave Naomi.

Read Ruth 1:16–17. Has anyone ever stuck by you so firmly, specifically during a difficult season? How did that affect your pain or grief?

Do you know anyone currently suffering the same type of trial you've experienced in the past? How could you support or comfort that person this week?

When we are going through difficult times, we must hold tight to hope in God and allow Him to comfort us during those times—through the kind words of a friend, a well-timed song on the radio, or even an unexpected sense of peace that comes through prayer or worship. Those experiences can then make us more compassionate toward others than we would have been otherwise. When we understand what it's like losing a loved one to addiction, struggling to provide for our family no matter how hard we work, fearing for the safety of our kids in our own neighborhood, or searching fruitlessly for treatment that heals our chronic pain or mental illness, we become more understanding of others in similar difficult situations. And once we have received the life preserver of hope that God offers us through His presence and His promises to never leave us even when life is at its hardest, ugliest, or messiest, we then hold in our hands a tool to help others. We might not have understood—or even cared—before, but now that we know what it's like to hurt so deeply and be comforted so abundantly, it's our responsibility and our privilege to walk alongside others in their pain.

A kind smile for the mom whose toddler is throwing a tantrum, a meal for a grieving friend, a grocery gift card, a few hours of free tutoring or babysitting, a visit, some flowers, or simply a listening ear—these are not small things. God can and will use whatever we can offer to those in pain (including our own difficult story), to remind them of His love and the hope that always remains no matter how hard life becomes.

Read Genesis 50:20–21. Like Naomi, Joseph had experienced many difficulties, but he also experienced God's faithfulness through each one. God's steadfast love through every twist and turn of his life made it possible for Joseph to show kindness and provide enormous help to many, including the very brothers who had caused him pain. How have you seen God use a bad situation for good? What good might come from a painful situation you're in right now?

SCRIPTURE MEMORY MOMENT

Test yourself on Psalm 23:4. Try to write it or say it out loud from memory. Because Psalm 23 so comprehensively tells us how to hold on to hope when life is painful, consider memorizing all six verses as you keep working through this study (or perhaps after you finish).

A PRAYER FOR TODAY

DEAR GOD, *thank You for coming alongside me during my most difficult seasons. Knowing You're walking beside me during the dark times is a gift I can barely comprehend. You are so good, and I want to share that goodness with others. Please open my eyes to any opportunity You give me to comfort others the way You've comforted me. Amen.*

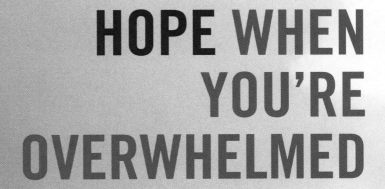

HOPE WHEN YOU'RE OVERWHELMED

Sometimes life isn't just hard; it's unbearable. We may have the best intentions to power through and stay positive. But when we are bombarded by one roadblock after another, slammed by one insult or injury on top of another, pressed in from every direction by responsibilities we can't meet, catastrophes we can't prevent, and exhaustion from dealing with it all—we can become overwhelmed.

Jesus acknowledges that we will have problems in this life (John 16:33), but He promises to be with us when they come. We can see this theme throughout Scripture, as the Lord vows over and over to be with us whenever we face difficulties. However, we're sometimes surprised when our lives are so difficult, and we begin to wonder if the presence of trouble indicates the absence of God.

This week's personal story of hope is a hard one. One of our (in)courage writers shares an honest look at the early days after her husband's death and how hard it was for her to cope with her increased responsibilities and deep grief. As you read, take note of how hope was her lifeline during those difficult days, and think about how God might offer you the same comfort through your hope in Him.

A Story of Hope

Bedtime was always a struggle.

On a normal day, putting three rambunctious kids to bed can be challenging. After my husband died from cancer, I was left as a young widow with three daughters ages two, five, and eight. Bedtime often broke me. It was like a neon-yellow highlighter stroke, a reminder that Ericlee was no longer there to help me. I was suddenly a single mom.

My husband and I were partners in parenting. We prayed for our family together. We agreed on discipline. We tag-teamed when the other person was tired or frustrated. Now I had to be the mother and father in parenting.

I finally got to the point where I had to surrender. There was no use trying to play the proverbial whack-a-mole game every night. As soon as one child was asleep, another one popped up and needed something. I was already emotionally wrung out and so were my girls. I prayed and made a survival decision. All three girls piled into my king-sized bed— the one I had shared with their daddy for eleven years. And now it was *our* bed. I held my girlies close at night and often let the tears flow. They struggled to sleep and so did I. Some nights it was hard to imagine a hopeful future.

I had always imagined my future with Ericlee. We had built a family, a ministry, and a community. We chased our dreams together. He was my coach, my confidant, my biggest cheerleader. We were supposed to grow old together.

It felt like my girls had been cheated out of time with their daddy. He wouldn't be able to attend their high school graduations or walk them down the aisle at their weddings. I feared his absence would damage them emotionally and their grief would overcome them.

In the quiet recesses of my heart, I had to believe that God saw me in this wilderness, in this grief, and that He cared deeply for me. He had a plan. I just didn't have eyes to see the details yet. And that's what hope is all about. Hope is believing what we cannot see. Hope is remembering God's faithfulness in the past and believing in His goodness in the present and for the future.

Hebrews 6 reminds us, "We who have run for our very lives to God have every reason to grab the promised hope with both hands and never let go. It's an unbreakable spiritual lifeline, reaching past all appearances right to the very presence of God where Jesus, running on ahead of us, has taken up his permanent post as high priest for us" (vv. 18–20 MSG).

I clung to hope like a rope that was rescuing me from an ocean of grief. These were uncharted waters for me. And day by day, God showed He was present with us. He was cultivating within me a heart of hope. He provided that lifeline.

One way I navigated the stormy waters was through a practice of gratitude. I kept a little journal and tried to jot down a list each day of the gifts I was grateful for. I wrote down the minuscule and the large-scale. I felt God's presence in the splashes of color waltzing across the sky each night at sunset. I heard Him in the made-up songs my two-year-old would croon in the car on road trips. I saw Him when that overflowing manila envelope arrived in the mail with money a church had collected to go toward our medical bills. I tasted Him in the home-cooked meals friends brought each night to see us through that hard season when even cooking felt like a heavy task.

He was my comforter, my provider, my husband in a time when I felt like I was swimming in stormy waters alone. As I learned to give thanks in the grief, I began to get glimpses of His glory. Instead of being fraught with anxiety, little by little I learned to breathe again. Each day was a step toward hope and healing.

It's been more than six years since my husband soared to heaven. I continue to be amazed at the doors God has flung open for my daughters and me. As we have clung to hope, God has given us opportunities to encourage other widows and their children.

God also brought my new husband, Shawn, to redeem our story in an unexpected way. Shawn was one of Ericlee's best friends. He was a longtime supporter of our ministry and frequently came to visit us through the years. Shawn was single, but Ericlee had a strong feeling in his spirit that God had someone special in mind for his beloved friend, so we had often prayed for Shawn's future wife. Of course, no one could have anticipated that God was preparing Shawn for me. He was the hope and future I never could have imagined.

Friend, if you are feeling overwhelmed and hopeless today, hear this: God is for you. He is sovereign. No matter what impossible situation you are navigating, He is working underground right now on your behalf. Cry out to Him. Trust Him. His promises are still true. Hold tightly to that rope of hope.

—DORINA LAZO GILMORE-YOUNG

Think back to a time when you felt overwhelmed—either with responsibilities and circumstances or with the weight of grief, anxiety, or other emotional burdens. Describe how that season made you feel (or how you feel right now if you're currently overwhelmed).

_____

_____

_____

_____

When you've felt overwhelmed by this world, how has God calmed the figurative storm for you? Did it happen when or how you expected?

_____

_____

_____

_____

Read Isaiah 43:1–7, paying particular attention to verse 2. God doesn't promise we will never go through a storm or face a fire; instead, He promises to be with us when we do and to keep us from being consumed by our feelings or circumstances. How does that promise give you hope in the context of your personal storms or fires?

SCRIPTURE MEMORY MOMENT

This week's memory verse is Isaiah 43:2. Write the verse in your journal (from the CSB as printed here or from your favorite translation). Throughout the week, commit these words to memory as you ask God to create in you a heart of hope when you are overwhelmed.

> *When you pass through the waters,*
> *I will be with you,*
> *and the rivers will not overwhelm you.*
> *When you walk through the fire,*
> *you will not be scorched,*
> *and the flame will not burn you.*

A PRAYER FOR TODAY

DEAR LORD, *life feels like too much today. Everything I'm facing and feeling is weighing me down, and I'm not sure if I can stand it another minute. Will You help me? Will You bolster my hope in You and remind me of Your promises? Show me how to hope in You, even when life is overwhelming me. In Jesus's name, amen.*

As evening came, Jesus said to his disciples, "Let's cross to the other side of the lake." So they took Jesus in the boat and started out, leaving the crowds behind (although other boats followed). But soon a fierce storm came up. High waves were breaking into the boat, and it began to fill with water.

Jesus was sleeping at the back of the boat with his head on a cushion. The disciples woke him up, shouting, "Teacher, don't you care that we're going to drown?"

When Jesus woke up, he rebuked the wind and said to the waves, "Silence! Be still!" Suddenly the wind stopped, and there was a great calm.

Mark 4:35–39 NLT

Think about the last time you were caught in a severe storm, whether at home, in your car, or even outside. Describe how you felt.

The story of Jesus calming the storm is told in three of the four Gospels: Matthew, Mark, and Luke. Each account describes a trip across the lake after a long day of teaching. Jesus—who was fully God yet also fully human—was understandably tired and took a nap. While He

> **God is holding us in His hand. He isn't asleep, and He hasn't forgotten about us—even when in our panic we've forgotten about Him.**

was sleeping, a great storm blew in. Just as the waves threatened to overwhelm the boat, fear threatened to overwhelm the disciples.

We often react the same way, don't we? We can become overwhelmed by external circumstances (relationship troubles, job loss, debt, too many demands on our time, parenting, caring for elderly parents) or by internal conditions (fear, anxiety, depression, anger, resentment). And when it feels like the winds of those overwhelming storms might knock us down for good, we frequently find ourselves looking around frantically. *Can anyone help me? Does anyone notice what's going on here? Who's in charge? Where is God in all this?*

For Dorina, she felt overwhelmed by both her life circumstances (single parenting, coping with the aftermath of her husband's illness and death) and her internal struggles (grief, fear of the future, anxiety over how she would deal with all of it). But rather than succumb to those waves and sink into despair, she reached for what she called the "rope of hope," trusting that God was still with her and working on her behalf even when she couldn't see or feel it. Unlike the disciples in the storm, she didn't begin wondering if God had fallen asleep.

> Psalm 121:3–4 says, "He will not let you stumble; the one who watches over you will not slumber. Indeed, he who watches over Israel never slumbers or sleeps" (NLT). Since we see that God in heaven does not sleep, what is He doing instead? Read the rest of Psalm 121 for some answers.

Read the following passages:

- **Psalm 139:7–10**
- **Isaiah 49:15–16**
- **John 10:27–29**

Over and over in Scripture, God promises to hold us in His hand or to hold our hands in His. Based on the promises in these Scriptures or your own life experience, what difference does it make when we rest in the knowledge that, no matter how overwhelming the world may be, we're in His hands?

Sometimes getting to a state of overwhelm happens gradually. Seemingly small (or at least not hope-stealing) troubles build up in our lives, our homes, our hearts until we snap under the pressure. Other times a figurative storm catches us off guard with a sudden, intense appearance. In either case, we can become so overwhelmed with fear or pain that we lash out, looking for anything to stop the storm. We might begin to seek solutions or solace from anyone or anything that offers a substitute for real hope or help. We turn to Google or Facebook, a punishing workout, or a numbing drink. All the while, God is holding us in His hand. He isn't asleep, and He hasn't forgotten about us—even when in our panic we've forgotten about Him.

We're not alone in these tendencies. Go back to Psalm 121 and read the first two verses. Though the psalmist is quick to conclude that his help comes from the Lord, he starts by asking, "Where will my help come from?" (v. 1). In Psalm 31, a psalm of David, he admits to forgetting where his hope is found. In the midst of a song about how trustworthy God is and how desperately he needs God, David also says, "In panic I cried out, 'I am cut off from the Lord!' But you heard my cry for mercy and answered my call for help" (v. 22 NLT).

Like the psalmists and the disciples in the boat with Jesus, we desperately need hope when life is overwhelming and we're tempted to panic and forget what's true. But while we're all going to falter in our faith at times, it's what we do next that counts. Will we spiral deeper into panic and doubt? Or will we acknowledge God's presence and power and turn our focus back to Him? These biblical examples are so helpful as they illustrate what happens when a child of God panics for a moment before remembering who holds us in His hand. Stories of people turning back to God and trusting Him, even when life is overwhelming, can remind us of our own hope and increase it.

Think about a time when you panicked before turning to God. Though you might be tempted to feel shame about forgetting even for a moment where your hope is found or where your help comes from, your story could be an encouragement to someone else in the midst of their storm! Write your story here, making sure to include both the doubt and the hope, and consider sharing your story with someone this week.

Let's return to the disciples and Jesus in the boat. Reread Mark 4:39. To stop a raging storm, Jesus utters just three words: "Silence! Be still!" These words echo Psalm 46, which begins with a familiar declaration of hope: "God is our refuge and strength, always ready to help in times of trouble" (v. 1 NLT). Toward the end of that psalm, God says, "Be still, and know that I am God!" (v. 10 NLT). We see a similar command even earlier, in the book of Exodus. As Moses attempts to calm and reassure the Israelites during their escape from Egypt, he says, "The LORD will fight for you, and you must be quiet" (Exod. 14:14). Other translations of that verse say you must "remain calm" or "keep still."

When we read these passages together, a clear picture is formed of a God who can win wars and calm storms with a single word. So even though our life may feel like pure chaos as we juggle (and drop) balls in our attempt to manage everything on our own, He is not just offering us a lifeline. He *is* our lifeline. He *is* our rope of hope when we are overwhelmed, showing us again and again that He is our best and only hope.

What do you need God to silence or still in your life? Take time today to get quiet and still, and ask Him to fight your battles or calm your storms.

SCRIPTURE MEMORY MOMENT

In Scripture, God never promises that we will not face storms, either figurative or literal. But He does promise to be with us. Isaiah 43:2 is a great way to remember that and to remember where your hope is found. Write the passage three times in your journal as you work on committing it to memory.

A PRAYER FOR TODAY

GOD, *thank You for holding me in Your hand, and forgive me for forgetting that my hope is in You. When the storms of life blow in, keep me mindful of the firm foundation You are in my life. Remind me of Your faithfulness and all the times You've proven trustworthy. Hold me tight, Lord, and I will hold tight to You. Amen.*

Jesus Christ is the same yesterday, today, and forever.

Hebrews 13:8

What are the constants in your life? Examples include a person, a place, a job, a home, or anything else that helps you feel secure.

_____

_____

_____

_____

In the final chapter of the book of Hebrews, the author covers a lot of topics, such as hospitality, marriage, and money. As he wraps up his encouragement and advice to the believers who would receive this letter, he quickly touches on all the things that can detract from one's spiritual journey. It's as if he's saying, "Don't be distracted. Stay the course. Focus on the main things." And one of the main things he comes back to is God's steadfast nature.

Hebrews 13:5 quotes Deuteronomy 31:6, where God says, "I will never leave you or abandon you." The writer then goes on to urge believers to remember their leaders who have spoken God's Word to them and not to be led astray by strange teachings. The most foundational truth is found in verse 8: "Jesus Christ is the same yesterday, today, and forever." Whatever else you're faced with and whatever else you do, remember that God never changes.

A lot of times when we talk about feeling overwhelmed, change is at least part of the problem. Unexpected and often unwanted change can leave us feeling as if we're tumbling through our days like a child rolling down a hill or a person riding a roller coaster blindfolded. Up is down and down is up. Hills and valleys come out of nowhere. We try to get our bearings and end up feeling dizzy.

When this happens, we can be tempted to grasp for anything within reach to stop the spinning and somersaulting. We pin our hopes on finding a "new normal," getting into a routine, or controlling all the moving pieces with spreadsheets and planners. Or we reach for something comforting—or numbing—to help us cope with the uncertainty, anxiety, worry, and grief.

In their deep sadness after the loss of Ericlee, Dorina and her girls reached for one another. Especially in the night, when everything seems a little bigger, a little darker, a little scarier, they needed to grab hold of someone, something to steady themselves. Of course, this wasn't a bad choice! But what truly grounded Dorina in that overwhelming season was her hope in God and all the big and small ways she saw His faithfulness in her life.

What life changes have been most disorienting to you? How have you seen God remain the same through changing seasons or circumstances?

_____

_____

_____

_____

> **Remembering that God never changes, even when everything around us (sometimes even everything about us) does, is the key to resilient hope.**

Overwhelming change and the burdens that come with it can cause us to feel confused, but we don't have to stay in that space. God's Word can lead us out and right back to solid ground. Back in week 1 we read Psalm 130, which says, "I am counting on the LORD; yes, I am counting on him. I have put my hope in his word" (v. 5 NLT). We can find hope in the Word of God, which Psalm 119:105 reminds us is a lamp for our feet and a light on our path. That's why Scripture verses like Hebrews 13:8 are crucial for finding hope when life is overwhelming.

Remembering that God never changes, even when everything around us (sometimes even everything *about* us) does, is the key to resilient hope. He is the same yesterday, today, and forever—which means that He is our true north when we feel ourselves tumbling out of control. And like the earth's magnetic poles, He remains the same no matter what storms we face.

Read Psalm 90:1–4 in the following translations: CSB, NIV, NLT, and The Message. (Use a Bible app or a website like BibleGateway.com.) Take note of the different ways God is described in verse 2. How does thinking about God being God from "eternity to eternity" or "everlasting to everlasting" change how you might respond to overwhelming circumstances?

What Bible verse or passage points you to true north and helps you find hope when life is overwhelming? Even if it's not a verse about God's unchanging character, if there is a verse that calms you during chaos, write it here. And keep reading below for more encouragement from Scripture.

While our human understanding of eternity is limited, acknowledging that God always has been and always will be provides so much hope when our own lives are weighing on us. But that isn't the only way God's Word gives us comfort and strength when we're overwhelmed. If you drew a blank at the above question about a specific verse that helps you, perhaps one of these can offer relief and remind you of the hope we have in God.

- "None of the good promises the LORD had made to the house of Israel failed. Everything was fulfilled" (Josh. 21:45).
- "We know that all things work together for the good of those who love God, who are called according to his purpose" (Rom. 8:28).
- "He will wipe away every tear from their eyes. Death will be no more; grief, crying, and pain will be no more, because the previous things have passed away" (Rev. 21:4).

From the creation of the world to when Jesus returns, from our very first breath to our last day on earth, God promises to be with us and to help us—and through His Word we see how He fulfills those promises. When we read about how He kept every promise He gave to Moses, Joshua, and the Israelites, our hope is strengthened. When we read about His promises to overcome the world and to wipe away every tear, we can hope in what we know He will do in the future. Even when our lives feel out of control, we can remember that God is the one weaving everything together for a good purpose—His purpose.

Read James 1:17. What good gifts have you received because God never changes?

SCRIPTURE MEMORY MOMENT

If God's Word is the source of our hope, then memorizing Scripture will prepare us to handle seasons of overwhelming change, fear, or pain. When those disorienting changes come, we'll be ready, secure in the steady hope of God, our Rock. Write Isaiah 43:2 in your journal again and read it aloud several times as you work on committing it to memory.

A PRAYER FOR TODAY

GOD, *You are my Rock, my Foundation, and my Hope. Thank You for being the one thing that never changes, even when the rest of the world is spinning out of control. I'm so glad to know You are in control even then, never changing and always loving me. I love You too, Lord. Amen.*

DAY 4

O Lord, God of our ancestors, you alone are the God who is in heaven. You are ruler of all the kingdoms of the earth. You are powerful and mighty; no one can stand against you! . . . We do not know what to do, but we are looking to you for help.

2 Chronicles 20:6, 12 NLT

What's your go-to coping mechanism when life gets to be too much? Do you turn to Google, social media, friends, a to-do list, or some other distraction to take your mind off things?

Jehoshaphat was a good king of Judah who followed God. When he was told that three armies had joined forces to attack him, his first move was to go straight to God: "Jehoshaphat was afraid, and he resolved to seek the Lord. Then he proclaimed a fast for all Judah, who gathered to seek the Lord. They even came from all the cities of Judah to seek him" (2 Chron. 20:3–4). Though he likely felt overwhelmed by fear of his enemies and the responsibility of leading and protecting his people, Jehoshaphat did not despair or succumb to his fear. Instead, he relied on what he knew and trusted; his hope was in the Lord.

Jehoshaphat gathered the people of Judah and prayed. He praised God's power and faithful love and then asked God for help, saying, "We do not know what to do, but we look to you" (2 Chron. 20:12).

Did you catch that? Before there was a fail-proof battle plan, before the path forward was made clear, Jehoshaphat called his people to prayer and praise. They acknowledged who God is and entrusted their overwhelming circumstances to His care. When the king could have wallowed in worry, he instead chose to stake his claim in hope.

In His goodness, God answered their prayers quickly, sending a messenger who told Jehoshaphat, "You do not have to fight this battle. Position yourselves, stand still, and see the salvation of the LORD. He is with you, Judah and Jerusalem. Do not be afraid or discouraged. Tomorrow, go out to face them, for the LORD is with you" (2 Chron. 20:17).

The people followed God's orders under Jehoshaphat's leadership, singing praises to God as the three armies that had come to attack Judah instead turned against one another until the entire enemy force was defeated at their own hand. Jehoshaphat and his people celebrated, giving God the glory for the victory. When facing overwhelming odds and fear, Jehoshaphat didn't panic. He turned to the God of Israel in whom he hoped. And just like Jesus calmed the storm that we read about on day 2, God protected the nation of Judah and then gave Jehoshaphat and his kingdom "rest on every side" (2 Chron. 20:30).

What battle are you fighting today, or what conflict or overwhelming attack looms in your future?

Who are you counting on to help you fight that battle? Have you asked God for help like Jehoshaphat did? Read his prayer in 2 Chronicles 20:6–12. What would a similar prayer for your specific situation sound like?

_____

_____

_____

_____

We've talked about how panic sometimes interrupts our hope in God when life is overwhelming. Another reason we might not choose to turn to or rely on God is because we think we should be strong enough to handle circumstances on our own. It's unlikely that you'll be attacked by enemy armies, but you might still feel as overwhelmed as Jehoshaphat when facing illness, financial strain, an intense workload at home or in your job, parenting challenges, too many meetings, a big project with a short deadline, caring for an aging parent or a child with special needs, or any number of problems you might be tempted to think you can manage on your own. You might feel like other people have bigger problems and you shouldn't bother God with yours. Or perhaps you feel ashamed that something supposedly small is weighing so heavily on you. Maybe you even think God has already given you enough wisdom or strength, so you should just figure it out yourself.

But what if God is telling you, like He told Jehoshaphat, "You don't have to fight this battle . . . the Lord is with you"?

In Psalm 147, we read that God does not expect us to be strong enough to handle everything that might overwhelm us. Instead, He honors those who trust and hope in Him. "He is not impressed by the strength of a horse; he does not value the power of a warrior. The Lord values those who fear him, those who put their hope in his faithful love" (vv. 10–11).

God responded to Jehoshaphat's demonstration of faith and trust by protecting and providing for him. Might He do the same for you—giving you wisdom, confidence in Him, and ultimate victory over your enemies?

Read the following verses:

- **Exodus 15:2**
- **Psalm 73:26**
- **Ephesians 6:10**
- **Philippians 4:13**

When you read over and over that God offers to give us strength, what does that tell you about His expectations of your own strength?

Throughout the Old Testament, God tells His people that He will give them strength for whatever they face. He doesn't tell them He'll eliminate their troubles but that He will give them what they need to overcome any trial. And throughout the New Testament we see many examples of Jesus's closest followers and friends confessing their need for His strength. It's evident that God knows how overwhelming this world can be—and that He is more than willing to help us handle it. No matter what challenges arise, we can hope in Him and lean on His strength.

Deep fear, devastating grief, or other tremendous burdens can cause us to become emotionally and physically weary. Constantly adapting to enormous change or chaos can just plain wear us out. So while we might want to find hope in the Lord during these times—both to survive in the moment and to move forward with confidence into the future He's planned for us—just the thought of reaching for our anchor can be exhausting.

Jesus knows that. He knows, friend! And that's why He invites us to take a break, to let Him carry our burdens, to rest in Him. In Matthew 11:28–30, He says, "Come to me, all of you who are weary and burdened, and I will give you rest. Take up my yoke and learn from me, because I am lowly and humble in heart, and you will find rest for your souls. For my yoke is easy and my burden is light." Even if you're not fighting a literal battle or facing an actual storm, Jesus is here to refresh your soul in the midst of the challenges in your life that threaten to consume you.

If you're facing debt, divorce, death, illness, infertility, depression, loneliness, unemployment, difficult relationships, hard parenting seasons, too many family or work responsibilities, or anything else that's just too much for you right now, Jesus is here—to take all the weight of it off your shoulders, to comfort you and guide you while you cope with it, and to ultimately save you for all eternity.

> Think of the thing overwhelming you right now. Name it specifically. Now imagine holding it in your hands or on your shoulders—and then picture physically placing it on Jesus's lap or at God's feet. You may need to actually unclench your fists or breathe deeply as you do this; let yourself feel the tension leave your shoulders and jaw. How does it feel to allow the Lord to take your burden and give you strength?

Dorina's strategy for staying grounded in hope during an overwhelming season was to adjust her expectations and practice gratitude. Jehoshaphat admitted that he didn't know what to do and asked God for help. What habit might help you stay hopeful when you're overwhelmed?

_____

_____

_____

_____

SCRIPTURE MEMORY MOMENT

Isaiah 43:2 features God's promise to be with us when we walk through the waters and the fire. Consider texting this passage to a friend who might also be encouraged by these words. As you work on memorizing this verse today, think about what your personal waters and fire have been and thank God for being with you during those trials.

A PRAYER FOR TODAY

DEAR LORD, *thank You for being here when I don't know what to do, when everything seems out of control. Thank You for being with me, for guiding me, and for protecting me. God, I pray that I will always seek You quickly when I'm overwhelmed, that I'll find my hope in You and You alone. Help me trust You to fight my battles for me. Amen.*

DAY 5

You will keep in perfect peace
   all who trust in you,
   all whose thoughts are fixed on you!
Trust in the Lord always,
   for the Lord God is the eternal Rock.
                              Isaiah 26:3-4 NLT

Have you ever known anyone who seems to remain calm in the face of overwhelming circumstances or positive even when everything is going wrong? What do you think enables them to respond like that?

_____

_____

_____

_____

Isaiah lived during a time of political unrest and was given the incredibly difficult task of telling the nation of Judah that they were sinning against God. For nearly fifty years, Isaiah was God's messenger, warning the Israelites over and over what would happen if they did not turn back to God. It seems a given that his task and his life felt overwhelming at times. And yet, you may have noticed that in this study on hope we've examined a lot of verses from the book of Isaiah!

In chapter 26, Isaiah praises God for all He has done and all He will yet do for His people. Verse 7 offers insight into Isaiah's understanding of where true hope comes from and his ability to cling to it even when people and circumstances oppose him: "But for those who are righteous, the way is not steep and rough. You are a God who does what is right, and you smooth out the path ahead of them" (NLT). Like good shocks on a car, going with God makes a bumpy road seem like a newly paved highway—smooth and calm.

Again, hoping and trusting in God didn't erase all of Isaiah's problems. His hope didn't push back the Assyrian army or convince the people of Judah to turn away from their idols and back to the one true God. It didn't remove the responsibilities from his life, either. What we see instead is that by hoping in the Lord, Isaiah was grounded in his faith—both in what God was doing in the present day and in what He would do in the future. Because of this, he was able to endure a grueling, thankless task for decades in a way that would inspire people for centuries. By fixing his thoughts on God and trusting Him, Isaiah was kept in perfect peace rather than panic and overwhelm.

> **Turn to Isaiah 40:28–31. Now that you know a bit more about Isaiah's life, take note of how many times Isaiah uses the word *weary*. What task or situation are you facing that's lasted longer than you expected or that's caused you to feel weary? How might your outlook or experience change if you were to stay hopeful?**

What practices might help you keep your thoughts fixed on God, even when experiencing overwhelming feelings or circumstances? Some possibilities might be regular time studying God's Word (hooray, you're doing it!), prayer, or talking with other believers who point you to truth.

_____

_____

_____

_____

_____

Nehemiah was another follower of God who faced a lot of hard times and still managed to lean on God for the most impossible tasks. He was living in exile and working as a cupbearer for the king of Persia. When Nehemiah heard that the walls surrounding Jerusalem had fallen and his people were unprotected, he was deeply grieved. Perhaps you can imagine how he felt if you've heard about people or nations experiencing incredible tragedy such as terrorist attacks or natural disasters. Simply confronting such pain can be overwhelming, not to mention discouraging when we feel unable to help. Nehemiah didn't stop at sympathy and sadness, though. Nehemiah 1:4 says, "When I heard this, I sat down and wept. In fact, for days I mourned, fasted, and prayed to the God of heaven" (NLT).

By hoping in the Lord, Isaiah was grounded in his faith. By fixing his thoughts on God and trusting Him, Isaiah was kept in perfect peace rather than panic and overwhelm.

After praying fervently, Nehemiah sought permission from the king to return to his homeland and rebuild the city of his ancestors and its walls. With the king's support, Nehemiah then traveled to Jerusalem, gathered a team of priests and leaders, and got to work. In Nehemiah 6:15, we learn that the wall was finished in just fifty-two days—which is even more incredible when you read about the opposition Nehemiah faced during the project.

Neighboring leaders and political opponents repeatedly mocked, threatened, and attacked Nehémiah and those building the wall. Read this passage from chapter 4 to see how he responded:

> When the Jews who lived nearby arrived, they said to us time and again, "Everywhere you turn, they attack us." So I stationed people behind the lowest sections of the wall, at the vulnerable areas. I stationed them by families with their swords, spears, and bows. After I made an inspection, I stood up and said to the nobles, the officials, and the rest of the people, "Don't be afraid of them. Remember the great and awe-inspiring Lord, and fight for your countrymen, your sons and daughters, your wives and homes."
>
> When our enemies heard that we knew their scheme and that God had frustrated it, every one of us returned to his own work on the wall. From that day on, half of my men did the work while the other half held spears, shields, bows, and armor. The officers supported all the people of Judah, who were rebuilding the wall. The laborers who carried the loads worked with one hand and held a weapon with the other. Each of the builders had his sword strapped around his waist while he was building, and the one who sounded the ram's horn was beside me. Then I said to the nobles, the officials, and the rest of the people, "The work is enormous and spread out, and we are separated far from one another along the wall. Wherever you hear the sound of the ram's horn, rally to us there. Our God will fight for us!" (Neh. 4:12–20)

When the task he'd been given and the world around him were surely overwhelming, Nehemiah placed all his hope in the Lord who had called him to this work. He told his people, "Don't be afraid! Remember the Lord!" He urged them to stay focused on God and on the work, reminding them (and probably himself) that God would fight for them. Despite literal attacks from every side, their eyes were certainly fixed on God and His call.

The Christian Standard Bible prefaces Nehemiah 4 with the heading "Progress in Spite of Opposition." In Nehemiah's case, progress meant building an entire city wall in less than two months. But in our case it could mean something smaller yet just as significant: trusting God when your bank account is smaller than your bills, relying on Him when a relationship is rocky or you ache with loneliness, letting His peace center you when your job or church or child spins out of control.

Nobody expects you to build a city, I promise. But take some time to imagine what you could accomplish if you kept your focus and hope on God. What difference could this kind of heart-strengthening hope make in your everyday life?

Through this week of studying the difference hope makes when life is overwhelming, how has God been working in your heart? How will you approach overwhelming seasons and situations differently moving forward?

SCRIPTURE MEMORY MOMENT

Test yourself on Isaiah 43:2. Try to write it or say it out loud from memory. As we move into the next week of our study, continue to reflect on this verse and the hope we have even when life is overwhelming.

A PRAYER FOR TODAY

THANK YOU, GOD, *for the men and women who have gone before me, giving me an example of what it looks like to follow and hope in You even when everything is overwhelming. Please keep my eyes fixed on You and give me strength to complete the tasks You've given me. You're so good and powerful; I know You'll do it. In Jesus's name, amen.*

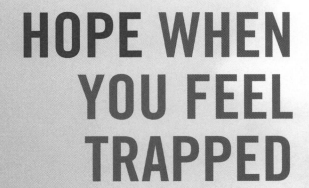

HOPE WHEN YOU FEEL TRAPPED

Sometimes life can seem so oppressive and our challenges so unending that we begin to feel trapped. Whether we feel trapped in a cycle of addiction or abuse, buried under the weight of unrealistic expectations or unmet goals, or stuck in the sins of the past (ours or someone else's), it's easy to believe we will never break free—that things will never get better, never change. We can even begin to think that we've maxed out God's patience, that we've outrun His reach or His ability to redeem what seems insurmountable to us.

But what Scripture tells us is different from what our broken, weary hearts say in those moments. As we've already touched on during this study, nothing can separate us from the love of God (Rom. 8:38–39). And we know that God promises to make all things new, removing all the old baggage that weighs us down and makes us feel trapped (Isa. 43:16–19). This is what (in)courage writer Anjuli Paschall shares with us this week as she tells us about how the shackles of a childhood spent hiding from conflict are finally being broken. As you read her story, start thinking about the things you fear you'll never escape. Ask God to open your heart to the work He can do in those stuck, trapped, or impossible places. Fresh hope and new freedom are possible!

A Story of Hope

Our conversation via text felt off. We were neighbors, and I would even call us friends. Alison was someone who watered our plants and fed the cat when we were on vacation. Our kids could play together for hours. Our casual connection over the years had always been peaceful.

But tonight everything felt different. Words were weighted, and the tone in her texts seemed loud, angry, and edgy.

I felt my chest curve inward and my lips tighten. My mind traced back through the events of the day. My gut reaction was, *I have to get out of this situation.*

I hate conflict. I freeze. I stumble. My hands shake. I feel like a failure. I'll do whatever I can to figure my way out of it. I'll take the blame, I'll sacrifice being right, I'll take the bullet, but please don't be upset with me. I come undone when others are disappointed with me. When I don't measure up to their standards of good, I come apart inside. I've always been this way. I'm an avoider.

When I was young and anger would explode around our dinner table, I couldn't breathe. I remember feeling small. Every slight movement I made was measured. My fingers pressed into my thigh and I'd look for protection at the side of my older sibling. Conflict was always big, out of control, and almost dangerous. I was left confused, cold, and wordless. I wanted to be strong, but everything in me felt weak. I was fragile. At any given moment I could break. Growing up I was always waiting for the ground to give out from under me. I had to stay above the water and made drastic and desperate attempts to stay afloat.

Even now as an adult, I use any device I can in order to not drown when even a hint of conflict appears. I do everything I can to make it stop. That evening, texting with my neighbor Alison, I used every strategy I knew to make the tension stop.

Our kids had had a physical confrontation that afternoon. There was yelling and cursing, and bodies had been thrown to the ground. Now the moms were trying to find a resolution. Our conversation moved from texting to in-person as we sat on Alison's sofa, a box of tissues between us. I felt my body go cold. *I can't do this*, my mind screamed. *I don't know how to stay in conflict without losing myself.* But I prayed. I reminded myself to breathe, and I pressed my fingernails into my leg. I listened. I cried. I tried to speak the truth in love. She listened. She cried. She spoke the truth in love.

Everything in me wanted Alison to be okay with me. I needed her to like me. I've spent my entire life trying to appease everyone. The subconscious soundtrack in my mind has always been, "Please be okay with me so I can be okay." But that's asking the impossible from the people around me; nothing they do or say can truly make me okay.

When I walked out of Alison's house that night, I knew it was just the start of more conversations. I knew the issue was not yet resolved. I knew she probably wasn't okay with me. But I also knew I was going to be okay. My worth, value, and internal strength weren't found in her liking me but in Christ. My security isn't found in being a perfect person. I let this truth set in. I can endure conflict because Christ is in me. Christ faced conflict until His death on the cross. Conflict isn't bad, and it even has the potential to lead me toward greater hope and healing.

I have struggled for years to escape the patterns of avoiding conflict that I developed during childhood, but God is working in me. Staying in conflict instead of scrambling to get out of it is painful, but I am growing muscles. I am learning how to swim, using the life preserver of God's love and strength to keep me from drowning. After years of feeling trapped by the wounds of my childhood and unable to move forward into healthier patterns, I see a glimmer of hope. I'm finally beginning to believe I won't always feel so fragile when confronted with tension or disagreement.

And I'm realizing that the goal isn't to be strong. I think that's where I've been wrong since I was a child. I don't need to be stronger. My fragility isn't a weakness. My fragility isn't a sign that I'm failing. Fragility is vulnerability. My fragility is what makes me wonderful. It is what keeps me close to my Savior.

I've often thought about Peter walking on water. I wonder if the liquid under his feet felt solid. Did it feel like he was walking on earth or mud or clay? Honestly, I think the water felt like water. It felt weak and incapable of holding his weight. It must have felt like he could slip at any moment. It wasn't about the water or even his own unsteady emotions. It was about who held him on the water. His hope wasn't in the stability of the lake or his ability to balance himself. Peter's fragility and the storm around him moved him to focus on Christ.

I can't place my hope in a lack of conflict or in people liking me. Hope is not found in my ability to control conflict or in strategies to escape from an argument. My hope is ignited when I stay connected to that fragile place inside of me and walk toward Jesus. Feeling fragile and even trapped is what keeps my gaze on Jesus. Conflict won't drown me. Pain from my past won't shackle me. Instead, they bind me more deeply to Christ. He goes with me, before me, and behind me. Even in the scariest places, hope is ever present. Perhaps I'm not learning to swim but to walk on water.

—ANJULI PASCHALL

When you think about feeling trapped or fragile, what comes to mind? Maybe it's an ongoing situation, relational dynamic, or pattern of responding. Perhaps you've been unable to break free from an unhealthy habit or to recover from a hurtful part of your history. Write down where you need God to work in your life and write a new chapter of your story.

Think about an experience that has had long-lasting effects or consequences in your life. Did you see God's presence then? If so, how? Do you see Him working in your life now?

_____

_____

_____

Read Romans 8:31–39. When you read that nothing can separate us from the love of God, how do you feel? Does that feel true when you consider your own situation? What, if anything, do you see attempting to come between you and God's love?

_____

_____

_____

_____

SCRIPTURE MEMORY MOMENT

This week's memory verses are Romans 8:38–39. Write the passage in your journal (from the NIV as printed here or from your favorite translation). Throughout the week, commit these words to memory as you continue asking God to create in you a heart of hope.

For I am convinced that neither death nor life, neither angels nor demons, neither the present nor the future, nor any powers, neither height nor depth, nor anything else in all creation, will be able to separate us from the love of God that is in Christ Jesus our Lord.

A PRAYER FOR TODAY

DEAR LORD, *sometimes I feel trapped and afraid that nothing will change. I start believing that my own shortcomings, the unhealthy patterns of my past, or my current circumstances will always be this way. But Your Word reminds me that hope is possible in You! Thank You that I don't have to be okay in the eyes of others to be okay. I am secure in Your relentless love. Help me to keep trusting You. Amen.*

Look, I am about to do something new;
even now it is coming. Do you not see it?
Indeed, I will make a way in the wilderness,
rivers in the desert.

Isaiah 43:19

What part of your life feels impossible to change right now?

_____

_____

_____

_____

Ezekiel was an Old Testament prophet tasked with telling the people of
Israel what would surely happen if they did not repent from their sinful
behavior. Using poetry and symbolism, he interpreted visions from God
into messages for God's people. He warned of severe consequences
for turning away from God in their behavior and in their hearts and
for worshiping idols. Indeed, just as Ezekiel predicted, Jerusalem was
attacked and conquered by another nation, and the Israelites were ex-
iled, sent away from their homeland.

Though Ezekiel's message was a grave one—a warning from God that was later carried out—he wasn't all doom and gloom. In fact, he preached immense hope, assuring the Israelites that God wasn't finished with them, that He would give them a new spirit and bring restoration to their nation. When it seemed as if their hearts and their futures were completely dead, God promised to give them life.

One of the visions God gave Ezekiel involved a valley full of dry, scattered bones coming to life. It's a wild image—and evidence of God's creativity! Read Ezekiel 37:1–14 for the entire story.

After such a strange vision, God didn't expect Ezekiel or the people to understand it on their own. He said:

> Son of man, these bones represent the people of Israel. They are saying, "We have become old, dry bones—all hope is gone. Our nation is finished." Therefore, prophesy to them and say, "This is what the Sovereign LORD says: O my people, I will open your graves of exile and cause you to rise again. Then I will bring you back to the land of Israel. When this happens, O my people, you will know that I am the LORD. I will put my Spirit in you, and you will live again and return home to your own land. Then you will know that I, the LORD, have spoken, and I have done what I said. Yes, the LORD has spoken!" (Ezek. 37:11–14 NLT)

Reread Ezekiel 37:3. How did Ezekiel answer when God asked if the dry bones could live again? What do you notice about his answer?

_____

_____

_____

_____

God made it clear that the dry bones living once again represented the Israelites who would be resurrected spiritually. What part of your life might need reviving today?

It's unlikely that we will ever see a bunch of skeletons come back to life. But it's quite likely that we will at times experience dryness or even death in our spirits. Though we don't literally die when our hearts break or our spirits give up, those experiences can feel just as permanent as death. When we can't seem to break free of unhealthy patterns that either we developed or others trained in us, when we can't find a way to restore a relationship or heal a wound, when we have searched and prayed and begged for help but still see no solutions to our troubles—we might just understand the imagery of dry bones after all.

The fascinating part of this story in Scripture is how vividly Ezekiel describes it. He is not vague about what he sees: human remains that had been exposed to the elements for a long time, now broken and scattered and covering the valley floor. This wasn't a fresh wound God was healing; it wasn't a simple nuisance or minor injury. It wasn't new, and it wasn't minor. The carnage God showed Ezekiel was the result of catastrophic destruction, and it had happened so long ago that just the bones were lying on the ground—discarded, beyond repair, without any hope of living again.

That's a pretty gross image—but it's even more devastating when it feels familiar to us. What do we do when our own situation resembles a valley of dry bones? In the book of Ezekiel, the Israelites had given up, saying, "We have become old, dry bones—all hope is gone. Our nation is finished" (Ezek. 37:11 NLT). They remembered their history, they

God promises not only to rescue us from captivity and exile (physical problems) but to renew our hearts and spirits (spiritual struggles).

couldn't deny their present situation, and they felt certain things would never change. Just like Anjuli, who assumed she would never be able to handle conflict in a healthy manner, perhaps you've feared that you will never get over a difficult situation in your own life. In the same way, the Israelites believed their lives, their nation, their future were hopeless.

But God loved them so deeply and so unconditionally that He essentially says, *You're not dead yet. This isn't finished.* As He assures in Ezekiel 11:19–20, "I will give them an undivided heart and put a new spirit in them; I will remove from them their heart of stone and give them a heart of flesh. . . . They will be my people, and I will be their God" (NIV). He promises not only to rescue them from captivity and exile (their physical problems) but to renew their hearts and spirits (their spiritual struggles). And He promises the same healing, reconciliation, and redemption to us.

Think about the areas of your life that you might describe as "dry bones." Which areas are physical problems and which are spiritual struggles?

_____

_____

_____

_____

Read Isaiah 43:19 again. Where do you need God to make a new way in your life today?

_____

_____

_____

_____

SCRIPTURE MEMORY MOMENT

Today's story from Ezekiel 37 reminds us that nothing is impossible with God. Think about the way He brought bones back to life when you practice memorizing Romans 8:38–39, which assures us that nothing can separate us from God's love. Write the passage in your journal three times as you work on committing it to memory.

A PRAYER FOR TODAY

LORD, _I know nothing is impossible for You. So even in the parts of my life where change or healing doesn't seem possible, I trust that You are still working. Please don't let my heart become like stone. Help me believe Your promise to breathe life into my soul no matter how hard or how long my struggle has been. Thank You, God, for working in ways only You can. I choose to hope in You. Amen._

DAY 3

He has removed our sins as far from us
as the east is from the west.
Psalm 103:12 NLT

Think of a time when you made a mistake so great that you were afraid it could not be fixed. How did your fear or regret affect the way you viewed God? What did you believe about God in that moment or season?

_____

_____

_____

_____

Peter was one of Jesus's most passionate followers and closest friends. Yet after Jesus was arrested, Peter denied even knowing Him.

> Now Peter was sitting outside in the courtyard. A servant girl approached him and said, "You were with Jesus the Galilean too."
>
> But he denied it in front of everyone: "I don't know what you're talking about."
>
> When he had gone out to the gateway, another woman saw him and told those who were there, "This man was with Jesus the Nazarene!"

> And again he denied it with an oath: "I don't know the man!"
> After a little while those standing there approached and said to Peter, "You really are one of them, since even your accent gives you away."
> Then he started to curse and to swear with an oath, "I don't know the man!" Immediately a rooster crowed, and Peter remembered the words Jesus had spoken, "Before the rooster crows, you will deny me three times." And he went outside and wept bitterly. (Matt. 26:69–75)

In that moment following the arrest of his friend and teacher, Peter was grieving. He was in shock over what had just happened and may have been afraid for his own safety. And though he was a man of integrity who loved Jesus deeply, his baser instinct of self-preservation took over. He turned his back on Jesus and lied to the people in the courtyard by saying he did not know the man. Not just in passing but vehemently with an oath. Not just once but three times. And as soon as he did, the rooster crowed. Peter grasped the gravity of his choice and instantly regretted it. He fled the scene and wept bitterly, his grief now multiplied with shame and remorse.

It's likely that you too have felt the sharp sting of regret. All of us have messed up at some point in our lives; all of us have sinned against God. And sometimes we can feel such overwhelming shame about our sin, or the sin itself is so damaging or deep, that we begin believing redemption is out of the question. We believe that we are too far gone, that we've done too much or it's been too long, that God surely has run out of patience for our wandering hearts. While Anjuli shared her story about struggling with conflict—a pattern that was a result of someone else's sin during her childhood and that she struggled to overcome as an adult—we can sometimes feel the same desperation and defeat that are the results of our own sin. Either way, we look at our situation and feel doomed to repeat a cycle or suffer consequences, certain this is our lot.

God has not turned His back on you, and He will not give up on you. Your sin cannot and will not separate you from the love of God.

Regardless of the reason we feel trapped, Jesus clearly demonstrated with Peter that we are never too far gone for Him. Let's turn to John 21. This chapter describes an encounter the disciples had with Jesus one morning after He had risen from the dead. The disciples had been on an all-night fishing expedition and were ready to give up when they spotted Jesus on the shore. He called out instructions to them on where to throw their nets for an abundant catch, and then they sat on the shore around a fire and ate together as friends. After breakfast, Jesus singled out Peter, questioning his love. Three times Jesus asked Peter, "Do you love me?" Three times Peter assured Jesus that yes, he did. Peter had denied Jesus three times, so Jesus gave him the opportunity to claim Him as Savior and profess his love three times.

Read John 21:15–19. Though Jesus does not say the words "I forgive you," do you think He did forgive Peter? What evidence leads you to that conclusion?

Read Matthew 4:18–20. We've noted the parallel between Peter's three denials and Jesus's three questions. We can also see the words "Follow me" repeated—first when Jesus called Peter to join His ministry,

and then when Jesus told Peter to care for His followers. Why do you think Jesus chose to repeat patterns and even exact phrases in this conversation?

Jesus knew the depth of Peter's regret, and God knows our regret when we are faced with our own sin. David wrote about God's intimate knowledge of us in Psalm 139, saying, "O LORD, you have examined my heart and know everything about me. You know when I sit down or stand up. You know my thoughts even when I'm far away. You see me when I travel and when I rest at home. You know everything I do. You know what I am going to say even before I say it, LORD" (vv. 1–4 NLT). God knows how desperately you wish you'd never told the lie, spoken those angry words, raised a hand, turned a blind eye to injustice or abuse, stayed when you should have left or left when you should have stayed. He knows what those choices have led to, the cycle you feel stuck inside. He knows how much you regret your poor choices and mistakes and how you feel completely trapped by the consequences and by guilt.

He knows, and He isn't walking away. God has not turned His back on you, and He will not give up on you. You may have sinned in big ways or small—though we know that no matter how we categorize it, all sin grieves God's heart. But that cannot and will not separate you from the love of God. Scripture clearly tells us this in Romans 8:38–39, our memory verses for this week. And today's verse from Psalm 103 tells us that if we repent, we will be lavishly forgiven. Peter's story proves this.

And this is where we find hope when we feel trapped by our circumstances, by the consequences of our choices or the choices of others, by our regret and frustration and desperation and shame. We find hope in a God who loves us too much to leave us in our mess. Our situations are never hopeless; *we* are never hopeless. We are not without hope. God has seen fit to offer us forgiveness through the sacrifice of Jesus, the one who never sinned (2 Cor. 5:21). He has promised to never leave us (Heb. 13:5) and to redeem what we have done or what has been done to us (Eph. 2:4–7). Though we may feel trapped, God promises to break every chain to rescue and redeem us.

What struggle or sin have you felt helpless to overcome? Today, ask God to speak into this situation, and let His love and care show you how to be released.

David begins Psalm 103 with praise: "Let all that I am praise the Lord; with my whole heart, I will praise his holy name. Let all that I am praise the Lord; may I never forget the good things he does for me" (vv. 1–2 NLT). As you reflect on the enormous gift and life-changing freedom of forgiveness that God offers us and His ability to redeem even the most horrible situations, take time to thank Him. Write down a few reasons you are thankful to God today.

SCRIPTURE MEMORY MOMENT

What a relief to remember that nothing can separate us from the love of God, not even our own mistakes! Take time to write Romans 8:38–39 in your journal as you ponder these verses today, and ask God to hide His truth in your heart.

A PRAYER FOR TODAY

GOD, *You know me. You know how horrible I've felt when I've messed up—and how afraid I've been that my mess could not be cleaned up. I'm so thankful for Scripture that tells me that's not true! Thank You for promising to blot out my transgressions, for forgiving me. If there is any unconfessed sin in my life, please bring it to mind so I can repent and invite You into that area of my life. Please go with me as I move forward, keeping my eyes focused on You and Your ways. Amen.*

DAY 4

When Jesus stood up, he said to her, "Woman, where are they? Has no one condemned you?"

"No one, Lord," she answered.

"Neither do I condemn you," said Jesus. "Go, and from now on do not sin anymore."

John 8:10–11

When have you faced the choice between turning from sin and continuing to sin? Which choice did you make? What happened?

In John 8:2–11, we read the story about a woman caught in adultery. A pawn in the religious leaders' attempts to entice Jesus into breaking Jewish law, this woman is brought into the temple courts and her sins are exposed before a crowd of people.

Then the scribes and the Pharisees brought a woman caught in adultery, making her stand in the center. "Teacher," they said to him, "this woman was caught in the act of committing adultery.

In the law Moses commanded us to stone such women. So what do you say?" They asked this to trap him, in order that they might have evidence to accuse him. (John 8:3-6)

Rather than playing into the hands of the scribes and Pharisees, Jesus uses this horrible scene as an opportunity to show mercy. He could have pointed out the cruelty of this display or their hypocrisy in threatening to stone only the woman, when the Old Testament law actually states that both the man and woman caught in adultery should be put to death (Lev. 20:10). Instead, Jesus simply bends low and writes in the dust. Only after every one of the woman's accusers walks away, unwilling to declare themselves sinless and throw the first stone, does Jesus address this woman.

We don't know what Jesus wrote in the dust; the Bible doesn't tell us. What we do know is that Jesus's words to the woman are not words of condemnation. In fact, He specifically says that He does not condemn her and then tells her to leave her life of sin (John 8:11). In the IVP New Testament Commentary on the book of John, professor and author Rodney Whitacre points out the significant difference between the religious leaders declining to condemn the woman and Jesus choosing not to condemn her.

[Jesus's] non-condemnation is quite different from theirs. They wanted to condemn but lacked the opportunity; he could have done so, but he did not. Here is mercy and righteousness. He condemned the sin and not the sinner. But more than that, he called her to a new life. The gospel is not only the forgiveness of sins, but a new quality of life that overcomes the power of sin.[1]

Can you imagine how that woman might have felt? Caught in the act of her sin—shock, vulnerability, panic. Pushed into the middle of a crowded room of religious teachers and leaders—embarrassment, confusion, shame, terror. As a woman with few rights who had been found breaking the law of Moses, she probably didn't hold out hope for rescue, much less redemption. Surely her situation was hopeless.

But God says no situation is ever hopeless. Whether we hope for physical rescue from a seemingly invincible threat, for eternal salvation through the saving work of Jesus, or simply for the strength to endure whatever we face, nothing can steal our hope when we know the Lord.

Think about a time you've been caught in sin, whether by your own realization or by someone else. How did you feel? If another person discovered or revealed your sin, how did that person react?

\
\
\
\

Read John 8:12, the verse immediately following this story. Jesus tells the Pharisees that He is the light of the world and those who follow Him will never walk in darkness. How have you experienced Jesus as a light when you've felt trapped by either sin or circumstance?

\
\
\
\

Sometimes the shame of sin is the thing that keeps us trapped—in a cycle of more sin, in despondency or apathy, in fear and hiding. That could have been the case for this woman, whose humiliation had been witnessed and judged by a group of religious leaders, a group of men.

But Jesus—this man who was powerful enough to silence the religious leaders and who was without sin—offered her both forgiveness and freedom. *I do not condemn you. You're free to go.*

And that's certainly been the case for many of us when we are caught in sin and feel too humiliated and remorseful to lift our eyes to Jesus and receive forgiveness. That shame can cause us to continue making bad choices, and it can lead us to hide from those whom we actually desire to be in relationship with—and from the very One who wants to free us from those burdens. Read the following verses:

- Isaiah 1:18
- John 3:17
- Ephesians 1:7
- Hebrews 8:12
- 1 John 1:9

Do you see? Our sins, our mistakes, our choices that lead us away from the Lord can wrap around our hearts and press down on our shoulders until we feel completely trapped, convinced nothing can improve our lives or our hearts and certain nothing will ever change. But God says that is absolutely not true! If we turn back to Him, He will break those chains holding us down! He will forgive us and free us from the burden of what's happened before. We can face ourselves, the world, and God Himself with confidence in the mercy, grace, strength, and peace He offers.

If you are feeling trapped, don't give up. God is still here. Nothing—no sin, no shame, no circumstance—can separate you from His love.

> **Ask God to examine your heart and bring to light the places you are trapped. As He does, ask for forgiveness and for freedom. Do you feel a difference? Describe here any changes you observe as you allow God to move in your heart.**

....

....

SCRIPTURE MEMORY MOMENT

Today as you practice Romans 8:38–39, take a moment to make it personal. Verse 39 (NLT) says "nothing in all creation" can separate us from God. What does that look like in your own life? Reflect on that as you write this passage on a piece of paper you can use as a bookmark in your Bible or in this study book.

A PRAYER FOR TODAY

OH GOD, *forgive me. You know my heart, and You know the things I regret. Thank You that Your forgiveness reaches even into my darkest places. Help me to move forward on the path You've created for me. Please erase the shame and guilt I feel about past mistakes and choices, and give me strength to handle any consequences that remain. Thank You for loving me enough to shine truth into my life and to rescue me from sin. Amen.*

May you be filled with joy, always thanking the Father. He has enabled you to share in the inheritance that belongs to his people, who live in the light. For he has rescued us from the kingdom of darkness and transferred us into the Kingdom of his dear Son, who purchased our freedom and forgave our sins.

Colossians 1:11–14 NLT

Think about a time when you found yourself in complete physical darkness. How did you find your way out? How did you feel as you navigated the darkness?

_____

_____

_____

_____

As we briefly touched on yesterday, Jesus says in John 8:12 that He is the light of the world. He says, "Anyone who follows me will never walk in the darkness but will have the light of life." Later, when Paul writes to the church in Colossae to teach them about Jesus, he says God's people, having been rescued from darkness, now live in the light (Col. 1:12–14).

It's actually not that common to find absolute darkness. If even a pin-point of light gets through, darkness is not complete. Still, we know what it's like to experience sudden darkness when the power goes out or when we wake up during the darkest hours and the night-light we keep in the hallway or bathroom has burned out. Darkness can feel oppressive, as if it's suffocating us. And it can mess with our depth perception and seem to go on forever. It's no coincidence that when God created the world, the first thing He did was create light (Gen. 1:1–5).

When Jesus explained who He is to the religious leaders of Israel, He described Himself as Light. As we read further in John 8, we learn how this Light (Jesus) offers freedom to those who follow Him.

> To the Jews who had believed him, Jesus said, "If you hold to my teaching, you are really my disciples. Then you will know the truth, and the truth will set you free."
> They answered him, "We are Abraham's descendants and have never been slaves of anyone. How can you say that we shall be set free?"
> Jesus replied, "Very truly I tell you, everyone who sins is a slave to sin. Now a slave has no permanent place in the family, but a son belongs to it forever. So if the Son sets you free, you will be free indeed." (John 8:31–36 NIV)

Darkness can hide a lot, including danger. Including sin. But when light comes in, those things are exposed. Jesus is the light of the world, and His light will shine on the things we've been battling in the dark. The sin we haven't confessed, the cycles we're caught in, the circumstances holding us down, the mistreatment or abuse we've suffered at the hands of others—all of it will be revealed by the Light. But unlike the Pharisees we read about yesterday, who brought a woman accused of adultery before a crowd for public judgment, God doesn't delight in punishment. He doesn't just shine a light into the places we feel trapped. He also shines light onto the way out. He is the Light and He is the way out. The truth of His light not only exposes our struggles but also sets us free from them.

All this metaphorical talk of light and darkness can feel a little vague. Read Psalm 119:105. That entire (long!) chapter is about God's Word, but this verse in particular explains how the Lord lights our way. How have you experienced direction or enlightenment through God's Word?

_____

_____

_____

_____

Reread John 8:31–36. What does it mean to you that you are no longer a slave to sin? Be specific and describe the difference it has made or could make in your life.

_____

_____

_____

_____

Someone who knew what it was like to be trapped, although through no fault of his own, was Daniel. After Jerusalem was attacked by the Babylonian Empire and the Israelites were captured and enslaved, Daniel and three of his friends (you may know them by their Babylonian names: Shadrach, Meshach, and Abednego) were assigned to work in King Nebuchadnezzar's palace (Dan. 1:1–7). Though they served the king faithfully and found favor with him, Daniel's friends found themselves in trouble when Nebuchadnezzar built a giant gold statue and commanded all the people to worship it. Because they followed God, Shadrach, Meshach, and Abednego refused—and their punishment was to be thrown into a fiery furnace (Dan. 3:1–23).

Later, Daniel found himself in a similar predicament. After defying an edict to pray only to King Darius, Daniel continued praying to the Lord God of Israel. His punishment was to be thrown into a den of lions (Dan. 6:1–18). A stone was even placed over the mouth of the den to ensure Daniel was good and trapped in that dangerous pit.

In both of these terrifying scenarios, the men were trapped in a seemingly impossible situation. No reasonable person looking at those circumstances would imagine any way that Shadrach, Meshach, Abednego, and Daniel could survive. There was just no way! Except these men served and trusted an almighty God—the one true God. The God who promises to make a way in the wilderness and rivers in the desert (Isa. 43:19). The God who is our light and salvation and stronghold (Ps. 27:1). The God Paul writes about when he says, "What then shall we say to these things? If God is for us, who can be against us?" (Rom. 8:31 ESV).

Unexpectedly and miraculously, Shadrach, Meshach, and Abednego were not burned in the furnace (Dan. 3:24–27), and Daniel was not harmed by the lions (Dan. 6:19–23).

> **Though we've talked a lot this week about being trapped by our own sin, that's not always what leads to feeling trapped in a never-ending cycle or an impossible situation. Have you ever felt trapped by circumstances out of your control or as a result of others' choices? Describe that experience here.**

God will give us the grit and determination, the peace and the faith to make it through our challenges.

Read how each of the kings responds to these rescues in Daniel 3:27–30 and Daniel 6:19–28. What was the result of God rescuing Daniel and his three friends (aside from the men's lives being saved)?

When we feel trapped, pressed on every side by the struggles we can't fathom overcoming or escaping, we can feel as doomed as someone thrown to the lions or tossed in a blazing fire. But when God's Word says nothing can separate us from Him, that includes lions and fire and anything we're facing in our lives today. Though we may not experience a complete elimination of the troubles facing us in this world, God is with us while we endure them. He will give us the grit and determination, the peace and the faith to make it through our challenges. And when He does, His light will not only guide us out but will also illuminate the truth for others.

Who do you think might be affected by your story of rescue and your testimony of walking in freedom and light? In other words, how might God be working in the lives of others through the example of His power in your life?

SCRIPTURE MEMORY MOMENT

Test yourself on Romans 8:38–39. Did you commit it to memory? Write the passage in your journal one last time and thank God for His unfailing love. As we move on to the next week of our study, continue to reflect on these verses and the hope you find in God's promises and plans.

A PRAYER FOR TODAY

THANK YOU, GOD, *for being an almighty God with the power to rescue me from anything. Thank You for loving me enough to do it. Show me the light, Lord, and set me free with Your truth. Open my eyes to any opportunities I have to share Your light and truth with others. Amen.*

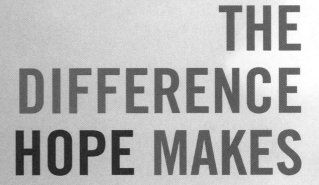

THE DIFFERENCE HOPE MAKES

We've reached the final week of this Bible study, where we'll take an extended look at the difference hope makes in our lives. Even for those of us who are naturally optimistic or are longtime believers in Jesus, we can find ourselves past the limits of our reserves when life hits hardest. When pain and problems are unrelenting or particularly brutal, we can lose our focus and our grip on the hope that normally keeps us afloat. And we can find ourselves sinking—sometimes so fast and deep that we aren't sure we can fight to resurface. But God refuses to let us go. As we've discussed over the past five weeks, He alone offers true hope, and nothing can separate us from Him.

Our last story comes from an (in)courage writer who has been dealt tremendous sorrow and struggles. She shares her experience of losing her hope and her will to live before remembering where her hope truly lies. She points us back to the truth of God's love and presence and describes the difference that made in her life, even when her circumstances didn't change. As you read Michele's story, think about what we've learned and about your own experience with hopelessness. How will this study—and what God has shown you—change you? Ask God to show you the work He's doing in your heart and how you can move forward more hopeful than ever.

A Story of Hope

I didn't expect to lose the will to live. That was something for quitters, those who were chronically negative or weak. From my earliest memories, I've always been a fighter. Determined, optimistic, stubborn to a fault. Quitting wasn't an option.

Until it seemed the only option I had left.

It took twenty years of consecutive, unrelenting losses for me to finally lose my will to fight. Betrayal, divorce, single motherhood. Remarriage, stepparenting, and adolescent parenting, followed by fostering and parenting three kids from severe trauma. Then came the three cancer diagnoses in the span of five years—bam, bam, and BAM. And in the middle of that I buried my dad after his thirteen-month war against terminal pancreatic cancer.

And those were just the "big" losses. There were other struggles that were less sensational but no less painful. Like a Weeble Wobble, I'd always been able to bounce back from a challenge. But after the third cancer diagnosis—the one that left me with a permanent disability and in chronic pain—I lost my bounce. Instead, I wanted to go to sleep and never wake up again. Any hope I'd once had was gone.

There's a verse in Romans 5 that talks about the power of hope:

> And not only this, but we also celebrate in our tribulations, knowing that tribulation brings about perseverance; and perseverance, proven character; and proven character, hope; and hope does not disappoint, because the love of God has been poured out within our hearts through the Holy Spirit who was given to us. (vv. 3–5 NASB)

And hope does not disappoint, the God-inspired Scripture says.

And yet I remember reading those words and immediately feeling a surge of resistance. And white-hot anger.

That's not true! I wanted to scream. *Hope* does *disappoint!*

I'd prayed for relief and deliverance for so many years. And yet, in spite of my bent knees and dogged hope, the only answer it seemed

I'd receive was more suffering. More loss. More grief and tears. Disappointment was an ocean, and I was drowning in it. I battled to keep my faith afloat, to believe in a good and loving and powerful God. And yet that belief only seemed to leave me weary and desperate for rescue.

Where was the God of hope? Where was the one who said He loved me and would always be with me? Didn't my relentless grief confirm His absence—or at least His disregard?

Somewhere in the midst of those hard years, I went to the mailbox and found a gift parcel. I didn't recognize the return address. Inside was a short letter from a total stranger along with an olivewood cross small enough to fit in the palm of my hand. In the following months and years, I found myself holding on to that cross and rubbing its smooth surface when the worst of the losses threatened to take me under. Something about its tangible presence brought comfort.

Then, during Easter one year, I finally understood why. Although I'd long celebrated Jesus's resurrection, it was Jesus's suffering that gave me hope.

Jesus knew what it was like to endure pain and loss. He knew what it was like to ask God for relief and deliverance and not receive it. For so much of my faith journey, I'd viewed Easter through the joy of Jesus's resurrection. But now I saw it through the eyes of His suffering and crucifixion. Jesus knew both physical pain and spiritual agony. He felt the seeming distance of the Father, who didn't intervene and spare Him the cross.

And yet Jesus didn't lose hope.

Why?

Because His hope wasn't in an outcome. His hope was in a Person.

> Remember your word to your servant,
>   for you have given me hope.
> My comfort in my suffering is this:
>   Your promise preserves my life. (Ps. 119:49–50 NIV)

Your promise preserves my life, the psalmist wrote. Not God's promise of happily ever after. Not God's promise of physical healing or a perfect family or pain-free existence.

But God's promise of *Himself.*

Jesus is God's promise fulfilled, divine presence in human flesh. And heaven—the hope of an eternal, pain-free promised land—is the final piece of that promise, when I will live in the hope-filling presence of my Father God forever.

It's now been almost six years since that season of suffering nearly took me under. I've had more hard days than I can count. Life continues to have unexpected circumstances and painful losses. Sure, I have plenty of good days too, and I celebrate those. But life remains hard for so many of us.

Still, as I look at my olivewood cross, more worn than it was six years ago, I remind myself again and again:

If I place my hope in an outcome—a prayer I want answered or a healing I want delivered—I will end up disappointed. "You will have suffering in this world," Jesus says (John 16:33). That's the bad news in no uncertain terms. None of us will escape the pain of the human condition. It's part of the deal.

However, Jesus didn't end with the bad news. "But take heart! I have overcome the world," He promises (John 16:33 NIV).

Jesus—the flesh-and-blood presence of God Himself—is our good news. He is our hope, our answered prayer to all prayers. And if our hope rests in Him alone, we will not be disappointed. Our hope is as sure as His resurrection, our eternity as perfect as His promise. One way or the other, my friends, the best is yet to come.

—**MICHELE CUSHATT**

Have you ever lost the will to live or the fight to keep enduring through a hard season? What led you to that dark place?

_____

_____

_____

_____

For Michele, an encouraging note and a small wooden cross redirected her focus to the suffering of Jesus and His resilient hope. What tangible reminders help you keep your hope in God rather than in a change of circumstances?

_____

_____

_____

_____

Read Psalm 43, paying close attention to verse 5. What encouraging words do you need to speak to your own soul about hoping in the Lord?

_____

_____

_____

_____

SCRIPTURE MEMORY MOMENT

This week's memory verse is Psalm 43:5. Write the verse in your journal (from the NLT as printed here or from your favorite translation). Throughout the week, commit these words to memory as you ask God to create in you a heart of hope, and see what difference it makes in your life.

Why am I discouraged?
Why is my heart so sad?
I will put my hope in God!
I will praise him again—
my Savior and my God!

A PRAYER FOR TODAY

GOD, *I am putting my hope in You. It's not easy, and I don't expect hope to act like a magic wand, taking away all my problems. But I trust Your plans for my life and Your promises to never leave me and to be with me when my heart breaks, for salvation through Jesus Christ, and for strength to endure through the Holy Spirit. Create in me a heart of hope that endures no matter what trials I face. I love You. Thank You for loving me too. Amen.*

Here is what I am commanding you to do. Be strong and brave. Do not be afraid. Do not lose hope. I am the LORD your God. I will be with you everywhere you go.

Joshua 1:9 NIrV

What is the hardest thing you've ever done? How did you see God moving in that situation?

In week 2 of this study, we looked at the story of Joshua. We noted that God promised He would be with Joshua and never leave him—and how after everything the Israelites faced, it was clear that every one of God's promises came true (Josh. 21:43–45). Today, let's go a little deeper so we can understand this story more fully.

Why was Joshua given the responsibility of leading the Israelites into Canaan, the land God had promised them? He earned it. When Moses and the Israelites arrived at the border of Canaan, they knew this was the land to which God had been leading them. Moses, in an effort to

Joshua and Caleb placed their hope in the Lord. And if God said it was possible, then they believed Him no matter what they saw with their own eyes.

move forward wisely, sent a dozen spies—a leader from each of Israel's founding families—to scope out the situation. He instructed them to determine if the land was good and fertile and if the inhabitants were strong and protected.

When the spies returned, they were scared. They had seen the Canaanites and believed they were too strong to defeat, so they lied about what kind of land it was. Rather than trusting God's promise that this land belonged to them and that they would be successful in any battle to possess it, they emphasized the size and invincibility of the people they would have to face:

> "We can't go up against them! They are stronger than we are!" So they spread this bad report about the land among the Israelites: "The land we traveled through and explored will devour anyone who goes to live there. All the people we saw were huge. We even saw giants there, the descendants of Anak. Next to them we felt like grasshoppers, and that's what they thought, too!" (Num. 13:31–33 NLT)

This report got the children of God agitated and anxious, and they refused to enter the very land God had promised them and led them to. Despite the strong leadership of Moses and Aaron and the testimony of Joshua and Caleb—the only two spies who reported the land was "extremely good . . . flowing with milk and honey" (Num. 14:7–8) and who reminded the people of God's promises to give it to them—the Israelites refused to move forward. God was not pleased and declared that none of the adult Israelites (except Joshua and Caleb) would enter the promised land. But He did promise that their children would possess it (Num. 14:30–32). You can read this entire story in Numbers 13–14.

Read Numbers 13:26–14:10. Why do you think Joshua and Caleb were unfazed by the size and strength of the Canaanites when they spied on them? What accounts for the difference between their interpretation of the situation and that of the other ten spies?

Read Joshua 1:1–9. The book of Joshua begins soon after Moses died and shortly before the Israelites finally cross into Canaan. Why do you think Joshua needed God's encouragement to lead the people into the promised land?

When the ten spies saw the large inhabitants of Canaan, their hope—which they'd placed in their own ability to fight—was dashed. Though God had promised them this land, they could no longer see how they could claim it. It seemed impossible, and they made sure everyone else knew it. Joshua and Caleb, though, had placed their hope in the Lord. And if God said it was possible, then they believed Him no matter what they saw with their own eyes. They urged their people to trust God, saying, "The LORD is with us. Don't be afraid of them!" (Num. 14:9).

But the people were afraid. Their hope turned out to be fickle, built on the shifting sands of their own understanding. They believed what a handful of men were saying about the situation rather than believing what God had said. Joshua and Caleb, however, kept trusting God, and as a result, they eventually moved into the promised land and enjoyed it.

Note the word *eventually*. Just because Joshua and Caleb's hope remained steady did not mean that their lives were easy or that they were untouched by the consequences of living in a broken world (and among disobedient people). And after forty more years of waiting, it didn't mean that the move into the promised land was smooth sailing. No, they still had to fight many battles—but they did not do it alone. God was with them, guiding them and protecting them the entire time, just as He'd promised all along.

> **Read Psalm 46:1–2. Note that the psalmist says God will protect us when (or though) the earth shakes and the mountains crumble. *When*, not *if*. As we've discussed previously in this study, God never promises a problem-free life, but He promises to be with us no matter what we face. How does that change your approach to tackling problems or moving forward, even against resistance or popular opinion?**

In Michele's story she shares some of the struggles she was facing when she lost her grip on hope (divorce, foster parenting, cancer). But she also notes that since renewing her hope in the Lord, she has continued to experience pain and loss. Her testimony and the story of Joshua both make it clear that, as Jesus acknowledged, we will have trouble in this world. But facing those trials confidently, knowing that God is on our side and promises an eternal victory no matter how many earthly defeats we experience, makes all the difference in the world.

For Joshua and the Israelites, it meant that the Lord guided them and protected them, allowing them to defeat the Canaanites and possess the land He promised to give them. For us it could mean that God sends us a friend to walk with us through a difficult season, leads us to an effective counselor or medication, protects us from the worst consequences of our choices (or allows us to experience and then learn from them), or gives us the mental fortitude and spiritual stamina to endure whatever comes our way.

When the time arrived for Joshua to stand and lead the people into the promised land—and into the battles necessary to take possession of their new home—God reminded him of the truth he needed to walk forward with boldness and bravery. May we hear the same words when we face our own trials: *Be strong! Be brave! Don't be afraid. Don't lose hope. I am the Lord your God. I'm always with you, wherever you go!*

What brave, hard thing is God asking you to do right now? Read today's verse out loud, but insert your name: "Be strong and brave, [name]. Do not be afraid, [name]. Do not lose hope, [name]. I am the Lord your God. I will be with you everywhere you go, [name]." How do those words encourage you to lean on God as you move forward in the difficult task before you?

SCRIPTURE MEMORY MOMENT

As we trust in God to be with us through every trial, let's not forget to praise Him for His faithfulness. Psalm 43:5 reminds us of both His promise to help us and our need to thank Him for it. Write the verse three times in your journal as you begin committing it to memory.

A PRAYER FOR TODAY

GOD, *please be with me—I know You are, so help me remember it and believe it! What I'm facing seems insurmountable, but I know that with You, all things are possible. Give me the strength and courage I need to move forward along the path You have created for me, and make me an example to those who are with me on this journey. Amen.*

Jesus said, "Everyone who drinks from this water will get thirsty again. But whoever drinks from the water that I will give him will never get thirsty again. In fact, the water I will give him will become a well of water springing up in him for eternal life."

John 4:13–14

Imagine how thirsty you might feel after walking miles through a hot desert without water. Now think back to a time when your faith felt dusty and dry. What quenched your spiritual thirst in that season?

In the book of John, we read a story about Jesus meeting a woman at a well and revealing to her His identity as Messiah. Jesus and the disciples were traveling back to Galilee to avoid persecution from the Pharisees in Jerusalem, and they stopped in the town of Sychar in Samaria. While the disciples went off to look for food, Jesus rested near the town's well. When a woman arrived to draw water, He asked her to give Him a drink. The conversation that follows between Jesus and the woman changed not only her life but the lives of everyone in her village.

Jesus tells the woman that He can offer her living water. Before He explains His cryptic message, though, Jesus tells her to go get her husband. When she says she isn't married, He then demonstrates that He knows her and her specific situation by pointing out that she's had not one but five husbands, and the man she currently lives with is not her husband. He then proceeds to tell her the incredible news that He is the Messiah, the one true God she and her people have learned about and waited for with great anticipation. The woman hurries off to tell the people in her village about meeting Jesus and what He'd taught her (John 4:28–30, 39–41).

The fact that this woman had five husbands is no small revelation. We're not told why this was the case, whether she had been divorced or her husbands had died, but we do know she was living with a man who was not her husband. The clear implication is that she was shunned for this. The woman's relationship history is likely the reason she went to the well in the heat of the day rather than in the cool of the morning or evening, which is when her neighbors would be there. Jesus's delivery of the good news to a woman known for her sin—and a Samaritan woman at that, since Jews traditionally did not associate with Samaritans—offers hope to each one of us who have also sinned.

Read John 4:28–41. What does the woman do after talking to Jesus? Why was this unexpected or unusual?

Read Mark 2:13–17. How does Jesus's statement that He came for sinners give you hope?

In the conversation between Jesus and the woman at the well, He never promises to restore her reputation with the people in her town. He doesn't claim that knowing Him will prevent the other women from shaming her or even make it more comfortable for her to draw water in the company of others. And yet, receiving living water from her Redeemer is so life-giving that the woman cannot stop herself from running back to town and telling everyone what happened.

Like we have discussed many times during this study, our hope is not in an earthly rescue but in a supernatural Savior. Our hope isn't wishful thinking that life could be different. Instead, it is confident expectation that God will fulfill His promises to never leave us, to enable us to endure the challenges of this world, and to save us from eternal judgment. And that is what empowers a sinful Samaritan woman to share the good news with her critics. Likewise, that is what gives us the motivation we need to boldly proclaim the goodness of God even when we face our own obstacles and heartaches.

Another encounter between Jesus and a known sinner illustrates the difference that hope in the Lord makes in a person's life. Luke 19:1–10 tells the story of Zacchaeus, a rich tax collector, which means he is someone who has cheated people out of a lot of money. But when Jesus seeks him out, Zacchaeus receives Him with joy and then promptly vows to give half his wealth to the poor and to repay those he had cheated.

Did that one public interaction and promise change Zacchaeus's repu-tation in the community? Not likely. Based on verse 7, which tells of the crowd complaining that Jesus was going to stay with a "notorious sinner" (NLT), it's reasonable to assume that repairing those relation-ships took time. But that didn't stop Zacchaeus from calling Jesus "Lord" and following His instruction to give to the poor.

You probably haven't had five husbands or worked as a dishonest tax collector, but you undoubtedly have faced situations—such as a dam-aged reputation, broken relationships, massive debt, chronic disease, or painful consequences from your or others' past choices—that will not immediately vanish or be transformed as your hope in the Lord deepens. But that doesn't mean nothing changes when God gives you a heart of hope.

Throughout the Gospels, Jesus consistently reaches out to the over-looked, the neglected, the outsiders, and the wounded. He goes out of His way to pursue conversations and relationships with people the world says are unworthy of such attention. Sometimes He heals what-ever affliction they are suffering, but not always. He does, however, always leave them with an overflowing, heart-changing hope. Though the problems we face today are often different from problems in the first century, we too can find unshakable hope even when our lives remain full of discomfort and difficulty. Jesus Christ, the Messiah, our Redeemer, is reaching out to each one of us, offering the compassion and living-water satisfaction we are longing for.

Jesus Christ, the Messiah, our Redeemer, is reaching out to each one of us, offering the compassion and living-water satisfaction we are longing for.

After reading the stories of the woman at the well and Zacchaeus, what similarities do you see in their interactions with Jesus? What about their stories gives you hope?

_____

_____

_____

_____

How has God been at work in your heart through this study about biblical hope? How could that empower you to tell others about Him?

_____

_____

_____

_____

SCRIPTURE MEMORY MOMENT

Both the woman at the well and Zacchaeus may have felt downcast about their situations, but a conversation with Jesus led them to joyful praise. Keep that in mind as you work on Psalm 43:5, and praise God for giving you hope even when you feel dejected, discouraged, or stuck in your circumstances. Write the verse in your journal, and ask God to write it on your heart too.

A PRAYER FOR TODAY

DEAR JESUS, *I am so grateful You seek out the lost and the hurting to offer hope and healing. I know that healing might not always look the way I expect or even want it to, but I also know that You'll be with me and love me no matter what. Lord, I love You, and I praise You for everything You've done and will do for me! Amen.*

I give thanks to Christ Jesus our Lord who has strengthened me, because he considered me faithful, appointing me to the ministry—even though I was formerly a blasphemer, a persecutor, and an arrogant man. But I received mercy because I acted out of ignorance in unbelief, and the grace of our Lord overflowed, along with the faith and love that are in Christ Jesus.

1 Timothy 1:12–14

Think about what you have already overcome and been forgiven in your life. How does that affect the hope you have for today and for the future?

_____

_____

_____

_____

You may have noticed that in this study we've spent a considerable amount of time in the Old Testament, specifically in the words of the prophets and the book of Psalms. Throughout the history of God's chosen people, the Israelites, their circumstances and choices frequently left them desperate and clinging to hope. Another place we find frequent mention of hope is in Paul's letters, which are found in the New Testament.

As we discussed in week 1, the hope we have is found not only in the possibility of rescue by an almighty God but also in the person of Jesus, who will save us for eternity, and in the Holy Spirit, the Counselor and Comforter who never leaves us. Because of all this hope, we are able to endure whatever challenges we face and to keep moving forward into the future God has planned for us. And as we will see in Paul's letters, hope should motivate us to good works and ethical choices as we follow the One in whom we find that hope.

Before we dive into those scriptural truths, however, let's review Paul's background. In Acts 9:1–30, we read of his miraculous conversion from being a persecutor of Christians to being a church planter. Paul claims he was the worst of sinners (1 Tim. 1:15); the book of Acts goes into a bit more detail, saying, "Now Saul was still breathing threats and murder against the disciples of the Lord. He went to the high priest and requested letters from him to the synagogues in Damascus, so that if he found any men or women who belonged to the Way, he might bring them as prisoners to Jerusalem" (Acts 9:1–2). Originally known as Saul, he was a Roman citizen and a Pharisee who was zealously determined to arrest and imprison Christians. But on the way to hunt down more followers of Jesus in Damascus, he encountered Jesus Himself.

> As he traveled and was nearing Damascus, a light from heaven suddenly flashed around him. Falling to the ground, he heard a voice saying to him, "Saul, Saul, why are you persecuting me?"
>
> "Who are you, Lord?" Saul said.
>
> "I am Jesus, the one you are persecuting," he replied. "But get up and go into the city, and you will be told what you must do."
>
> The men who were traveling with him stood speechless, hearing the sound but seeing no one. Saul got up from the ground, and though his eyes were open, he could see nothing. So they took him by the hand and led him into Damascus. He was unable to see for three days and did not eat or drink. (Acts 9:3–9)

In that single encounter, Saul was transformed into a passionate follower of Jesus. Though the disciples were initially and understandably wary, God provided Saul with friends and counselors and a new mission: spreading the good news of Jesus to whoever would listen. Saul appreciated having his physical sight restored by Ananias, but he was even more grateful to gain spiritual sight! Saul now knew the truth and committed to teaching others the very way of Jesus that he had previously scorned and attacked.

> **Read Acts 7:54–8:3 (a glimpse of Saul before he met Jesus) and Acts 9:10–23 (the story of Saul's conversion to faith in Jesus). Describe the differences you see in this one man. (Remember, Saul was later called Paul.)**

What role do you think hope played in the changes we see in Paul?

As Paul traveled—gathering with believers, teaching them the way of Jesus, and starting new churches—he wrote many letters. His letters include both theological teachings about the divine nature of Jesus as well as practical wisdom about how to conduct oneself as a follower and representative of Christ. Frequently, that behavior is described as a natural outpouring of the hope believers find in the Lord.

Read the following verses:

- **Romans 15:13–14**
- **Colossians 1:3–6**
- **1 Timothy 4:7–10**
- **Titus 2:11–15**

Which of these passages resonates most with you today? Describe what our hope in God will enable or compel us to do, according to one or two of these passages.

_____

_____

_____

_____

How has hope allowed or motivated you to be self-controlled, say no to "godless living and sinful pleasures," love God's people, and teach others about Jesus? If this hasn't been your experience, describe instead the fruit you see of the hope you have.

_____

_____

_____

_____

When we read about Saul before his conversion to Christianity, it seems that his only purpose was persecution, and his hope may have simply been in his ability to rid the nation of as many Christians as possible. As we read more of his story in Acts and his letters throughout the New Testament, it is clear that his purpose changed just as dramatically as his hope did.

While your own conversion from cynical unbelief to hopeful belief may not be as dramatic as Paul's and you may not feel called to travel, speak, and write publicly about Jesus, it's clear that you will be asked to live differently because of the hope you find in God's promises and plans, in salvation through Jesus, and in the comfort and counsel of the Holy Spirit. That hope might prompt you to volunteer for a ministry or charity, read Bible stories to your children, forgive your neighbors who wake you up with loud music at night, move far from home to serve others, or stay in a friendship that tests your patience. Hope-inspired actions will look different for each of us, but they will have in common their ability to point others to God. May we be open to learning how God can use our overflowing hope in our lives and in the lives of others.

SCRIPTURE MEMORY MOMENT

Praise God for the hope you have in Him today while you work on memorizing Psalm 43:5. Write the verse on a sticky note and place it in a prominent place where you'll see it frequently.

A PRAYER FOR TODAY

GOD, *thank You so much for the hope You've given me! It's such a tremendous gift, and I want others to know about it too. Please use me to spread the good news of the glorious hope You offer us. Amen.*

DAY 5

You have turned my mourning into joyful dancing.
　　You have taken away my clothes of mourning and clothed
　　　　me with joy,
that I might sing praises to you and not be silent.
　　O LORD my God, I will give you thanks forever!

Psalm 30:11-12 NLT

How have you seen God show up in your life after you asked for His help?

_____

_____

_____

_____

David was chosen by God to rule the nation of Israel. He was a shepherd, a giant-slayer, a songwriter, and a devoted friend. He is often remembered as a man after God's own heart (1 Sam. 13:14). And yet he did not lead a charmed, easy life nor was he blameless. David was attacked and hunted by jealous King Saul. One of his own sons betrayed him, two of his sons were murdered, and another son died in infancy. And we must also acknowledge that David raped a woman and had her husband killed. To say David's life was complicated is an understatement!

Many of the psalms David wrote give us significant insight into his circumstances, his reaction to the consequences, and his relationship with God. Read the following passages for a peek into David's journey:

- Psalm 25:4–7
- Psalm 51:10–13
- Psalm 59:1–4

Whether he was scared, sad, or remorseful, David turned to God. Though he commanded large armies and ruled an entire nation, his hope remained securely in the Lord. Though he had defeated a giant with just a slingshot and a small stone, he knew his strength came from God and only God. David hoped in the Lord to help him endure astonishing hardships. He hoped in God and trusted the future He would provide.

What do you take away from reading about David's life and his commitment to placing his hope in God?

Isaiah 49:23 says, "Those who put their hope in me will not be put to shame." When you reflect on David's life and his persistent hope, what does this truth from Isaiah mean to you?

_____

_____

_____

David enjoyed God's forgiveness and mercy, His rescue and provision many times over. But that doesn't mean his story ended happily ever after. All the ragged threads of consequences weren't tied up into a neat bow. Though David repented after committing adultery with Bathsheba (2 Sam. 11:2–5) and arranging for her husband to be killed (11:6–17), the son he had with Bathsheba died in infancy (12:13–19). Though God chose Solomon, one of David's sons, to rule as king after him, two of David's other sons were guilty of rape, incest, murder, and insurrection. And in the end, David was not allowed the honor of building the temple of God.

In 2 Samuel 7, we read that David wanted to build a new dwelling place for the Lord. This was a noble desire, but God sent a message through the prophet Nathan saying that He had not asked David to build Him a house. God went on to say that, while David would not be allowed to build God's temple, his son would be given the task instead. (Read 1 Chronicles 28, where David explains this to the people and hands over the temple plans to his son Solomon.)

Think about a time you experienced the consequences of your choices. How did you see God in that experience?

_____

_____

_____

_____

_____

> **Having hope in God will never let you down. Instead, it will turn your mourning into dancing and fill your heart with peace and joy.**

Let's read all of Psalm 30. David expresses such gratitude and love for God and what He has done for him. But what's most interesting is that this psalm was written as a dedication for the temple—the temple that David longed to build but was not allowed to build. David could have been bitter and resentful that his son would be the one building the temple. He could have argued with God and tried to do it anyway, forcing his own will. Instead, he trusted God's plan, submitted himself to God's ways, and rejoiced in God's faithfulness.

Even though we're reaching the end of our study on hope, your situation may still feel overwhelming, as if you're trapped in a place you don't want to be. You may still be waiting or feel deeply hurt. But even in those places, God is with you. And even when you aren't rescued right away, He promises to finish the work He's begun in you (Phil. 1:6). He is steady and faithful and fulfills every promise (2 Cor. 1:20). Having hope in Him will never let you down. Instead, it will turn your mourning into dancing and fill your heart with peace and joy.

May you put your hope in God, praising Him as your Lord and Savior and living out what you've learned in this study. May you remember that He loves you, He is always with you, and He has great plans for you. May the Lord God continue creating a hopeful heart in you.

What truth about hope will you take with you as we complete this study?

_____

_____

SCRIPTURE MEMORY MOMENT

Test yourself on Psalm 43:5. Try to write it or say it out loud from memory. Take time to meditate on all six of the passages we've memorized in this study, especially when you need God to create a heart of hope in you.

A PRAYER FOR TODAY

DEAR GOD, *thank You for moving in my heart over the past several weeks. I praise You for being a faithful Father who never leaves me and always makes a way for me. Help me commit these truths to my heart and share my overflowing hope with others who need You just as much as I do. My heart is Yours. My life is Yours. Keep writing Your story of hope through me. Amen.*

NOTES

Week 1 What Is Hope?

1. William B. Nelson Jr., "Hope," *Baker's Evangelical Dictionary of Biblical Theology*, ed. Walter A. Elwell (Grand Rapids: Baker Books, 1996) https://www.biblestudytools.com/dictionary/hope/.

2. John Piper, "What Is So Important About Christian Hope?," Desiring God, March 7, 2008, https://www.desiringgod.org/interviews/what-is-so-important-about-christian-hope.

3. Charles Haddon Spurgeon, "The Cure for a Weak Heart" (sermon), March 4, 1886, Metropolitan Tabernacle Pulpit, vol. 42, https://www.spurgeon.org/resource-library/sermons/the-cure-for-a-weak-heart/#flipbook/.

4. Edward Mote (1797–1874), "My Hope Is Built on Nothing Less" (1834), Hymnary.org, https://hymnary.org/text/my_hope_is_built_on_nothing_less.

5. Piper, "What Is So Important About Christian Hope?"

6. Matthew Henry, "Hebrews 6," *Matthew Henry Commentary on the Whole Bible*, Bible Study Tools, https://www.biblestudytools.com/commentaries/matthew-henry-complete/hebrews/6.html.

Week 3 Hope When You're Hurt

1. Gerald H. Wilson, *Psalms—Volume 1*, NIV Application Commentary (Grand Rapids: Zondervan, 2002), https://www.biblegateway.com/resources/nivac-sample/Ps.23.4.

Week 5 Hope When You Feel Trapped

1. Rodney A. Whitacre, *John*, IVP New Testament Commentary Series, ed. Grant R. Osborne (Downers Grove, IL: IVP Academic, 2010), https://www.biblegateway.com/resources/ivp-nt/Jesus-Forgives-Woman-Taken.

ABOUT THE AUTHORS

Mary Carver is a writer and speaker who lives for good books, spicy queso, and television marathons—but lives because of God's grace. She writes about giving up on perfect and finding truth in unexpected places at www.MaryCarver.com and on Instagram @marycarver. Mary and her husband live in Kansas City with their two daughters.

Michele Cushatt is a storyteller at heart who writes and speaks on the importance of perseverance, leadership, and faith in the hard places. A three-time tongue cancer survivor and mama to children "from hard places," Michele is a (reluctant) expert on pain, trauma, and our deep human need for real connection. She lives in Colorado with her husband and their six children, ages fourteen to twenty-nine. Find out more about Michele at www.MicheleCushatt.com.

Holley Gerth is a *Wall Street Journal* bestselling author, counselor, and life coach. Her newest release is *What Your Soul Needs for Stressful Times: 60 Powerful Truths to Protect Your Peace*. She's also wife to Mark, Mom to Lovelle, and Nana to Eula and Clem. Connect with her or learn more at www.HolleyGerth.com.

Dorina Lazo Gilmore-Young is passionate about helping people chase God's glory on life's unexpected trails and flourish in their

God-given callings. Dorina has published children's books, Bible studies, poetry, and just released her first devotional, *Walk Run Soar*. She and her husband, Shawn, started the Glory Chasers Christian running group, are hosts of the *Walk Run Soar* podcast, and together are raising three brave daughters in Central California. Connect with her at www.DorinaGilmore.com.

Aliza Latta is a Canadian writer, artist, and author who is a huge fan of telling stories. Her artwork and writing have been featured in publications for LifeWay, Dayspring, and (in)courage. She is always searching for the goodness of God, even when she has to squint to see it. Connect with her online through www.AlizaLatta.com or on Instagram @alizalatta.

Anjuli Paschall is the author of *Stay: Discovering Grace, Freedom, and Wholeness Where You Never Imagined Looking*. Growing up as a missionary kid, she secretly wondered, "Why does everyone else but me understand what a relationship with Jesus is?" It wasn't until she ran into her fears instead of from them that Anjuli found her voice and the love of God meeting her there. She is a pastor's wife, spiritual director, writer, and mom to five kids. Connect with her online at www.AnjuliPaschall.com or on Instagram @lovealways.anjuli.

(in)courage welcomes you

to a place where authentic, brave women connect deeply with God and others. Through the power of shared stories and meaningful resources, (in)courage champions women and celebrates the strength Jesus gives to live out our calling as God's daughters. Together we build community, celebrate diversity, and **become women of courage.**

Join us at **www.incourage.me**
and connect with us on social media!

100 Days of Hope and Peace

In this 100-day devotional, the (in)courage community reaches into the grief and pain of both crisis and ordinary life. Each day includes a key Scripture, a heartening devotion, and a prayer to remind you that God is near and hope is possible. You won't find tidy bows or trite quick fixes, just arrows pointing you straight to Jesus.

Revell
a division of Baker Publishing Group
www.RevellBooks.com

Available wherever books and ebooks are sold.

Bible Studies to Refresh Your Soul

In these six-week Bible studies, your friends at (in)courage will help you dive deep into real-life issues, the transforming power of God's Word, and what it means to courageously live your faith.

Available wherever books and ebooks are sold.

New Women's Bible Study Series from the (in)courage Community

This six-week Bible study series from (in)courage pairs Scripture with story, inviting us into a deeper experience of God's Word. Packed with solid observation, interpretation, and application of Scripture, plus daily prayers and memorization, each study strengthens the partnership between us and God.